RAISING KIDS RIGHT

Refreshingly simple advice to help take the frustration out of raising children

Karen Robertson

REVIEW AND HERALD® PUBLISHING ASSOCIATION
HAGERSTOWN, MD 21740

Copyright © 1998 by
Review and Herald® Publishing Association
International copyright secured

The author assumes full responsibility for the accuracy of all facts and quotations as cited in this book.

Scripture quotations marked NASB are from the *New American Standard Bible,* © The Lockman Foundation 1960, 1962, 1963, 1968, 1971, 1972, 1973, 1975, 1977.

This book was
Edited by Jeannette R. Johnson
Copyedited by James Cavil
Designed by GenesisDesign/Bryan Gray
Cover photo by PhotoDisc
Typeset: 11/13 Stone Serif

PRINTED IN U.S.A.

02 01 00 99 98   5 4 3 2 1

R&H Cataloging Service
Robertson, Karen A. 1942-
    Raising kid's right.

    1. Child rearing. I. Title.

            649.1

ISBN 0-8280-1295-4

To order additional copies of *Raising Kids Right,* by Karen Robertson, call 1-800-765-6955. Visit us at www.rhpa.org for more information on Review and Herald products.

DEDICATION

To my husband, Barry...
    for loving me, unconditionally,
    for allowing me to be myself (even when I'm
        Ditzi, the clown),
    and for accepting the challenge of raising my children
        as his own.

And to Jason and Jodi . . .
    who responded positively to our parenting and agreed
        to let me share their lives in this book.

ACKNOWLEDGMENTS

A special thanks to my daughter-in-law, Cecillia, who is always willing to proofread and critique my writing; to Marita Littauer, who offered lots of opportunities for me to grow as a speaker and writer; to Dorothy Comm, Olivine Bohner, and Jo Peck, my critique partners, who listened patiently to every chapter; and to Mom and Dad, Garnet and Hank Brassfield, who sacrificed to give me the experiences I needed to succeed in life.

CONTENTS

PREFACE

INTRODUCTION

CHAPTER 1   Good Morning!........................... 15

CHAPTER 2   Whose Turn in the Bathroom?............. 17

CHAPTER 3   I Don't Have a Thing to Wear............. 20

CHAPTER 4   What's for Breakfast?..................... 26

CHAPTER 5   What's on TV?........................... 30

CHAPTER 6   Clean Up Your Room..................... 33

CHAPTER 7   Where Are Your Books?................... 37

CHAPTER 8   'Bye, Kids; See You Later................. 39

CHAPTER 9   Don't Be Late!........................... 42

CHAPTER 10 An Apple for the Teacher?................ 44

CHAPTER 11 How Can I Help?........................ 48

CHAPTER 12 Did You Wash Behind Your Ears?.......... 51

CHAPTER 13 What's for Lunch?....................... 53

CHAPTER 14 It's a Bitter Pill to Swallow............... 55

CHAPTER 15 Cat Got Your Tongue?................... 57

CHAPTER 16	You're Dismissed	59
CHAPTER 17	Free Time?	62
CHAPTER 18	Fitting Friends?	73
CHAPTER 19	"Mom, Tell Jason to Stop Buggin' Me!"	76
CHAPTER 20	Are You Listening to Me?	80
CHAPTER 21	What Are You Listening To?	82
CHAPTER 22	Have You Done Your Chores?	84
CHAPTER 23	What's for Dinner?	86
CHAPTER 24	In Case of an Emergency	89
CHAPTER 25	Have You Finished Your Homework?	91
CHAPTER 26	Nighttime TV?	95
CHAPTER 27	Family Meetings	97
CHAPTER 28	Let's Read Together	99
CHAPTER 29	Now I Lay Me Down to Sleep	102
CHAPTER 30	Can We Read a Little More?	106
CHAPTER 31	God Bless One and All	109
EPILOGUE		111

PREFACE

This is a "Feel Good Parenting Manual," written for every parent who has school-age children, kindergarten through grade 8.

Raising children is a serious business, but it can be fun if you do it right. It is never easy, because it takes constant attention from "rise and shine" to "lights out."

It's not a job you can take a vacation from or give to someone else. And even if you mess it up, you will never get fired. Living with your mistakes, however, can be worse.

God gave us children; let us make the best of them!

INTRODUCTION

I've used up all my excuses: The kids are raised, I'm out of the classroom, the credentials are on the wall. I'm sitting at a beautiful oak rolltop desk in front of a new computer my husband, Barry, bought for me.

This book, a simple, step-by-step instruction book for working parents (all parents work, whether at home or away), is *my* responsibility.

No one made me do it, but I had 10 reasons for writing this book:

1. Children don't come with instructions.

When I went to school, I learned how to read maps, execute mathematical calculations, identify birds, write research papers, make speeches, and use reference material to find information I couldn't get anywhere else. However, classes on the art of raising children did not exist.

Every student took driver's training in anticipation of climbing behind the wheel of a car at age 16. A big day, it's true, but nothing compared to the birth of a child. Doesn't it seem strange that not one class was available in parenting, even though most of us expected to be parents someday?

2. A unique approach makes this book different from all the others.

Each chapter covers a situation faced by parents nearly every day, with suggestions in the Try This section at the end of each chapter. The first chapter of the book opens with the morning greeting, and the last chapter ends with the evening prayer. This book is a step-by-step, through-the-day manual for every parent of K-8 children, single or married.

3. This primer can make parenting easier.

It seems a shame to have spent more than 25 years learning something unless I can pass it on to others. That must be the teacher in me! ("The aged women . . . may teach the young women . . . to love their children" [Titus 2:3].) The trick is to raise children who are lovable.

This book contains what I learned about parenting in my 30 years as a parent and a teacher. I hope it will help mothers and fathers everywhere to raise kids who will bless them all the days of their lives.

4. I've tried to simplify the best of the best.

During my child-rearing years I read books by James Dobson, Haim Ginot, and others. I took ideas from each teacher and asked God to guide me. I'm grateful for the writings that were a help to me, and I want to give to others. I thank God that I have come to this time in my life when my children have become successful adults, brothers and sisters in Christ, and friends.

5. I have credentials.

I raised my two children and helped with more than 800 others who came through my classes, played on my teams, or rode with us to sporting events. I wish I could say that I have all the answers, but I don't.

As a parent I know what worked for us, and I've learned from the mistakes we made. As a teacher I saw the results of others' parenting, some good and some bad. Many of my students were really my teachers on the subject—my master's degree in counseling is insignificant compared to what I learned from the children.

6. My kids made me do it.

Jason, our older, said, "Mom, when I have kids, I hope

I can raise them just like you raised us, because I think we turned out to be pretty good people." Nothing wrong with *his* ego!

Our daughter, Jodi, drove me to my first professional speaking engagement. I was nervous and silent as we drove along. When the presentation was over and we were returning to the car, she stated simply, "You're pretty good. For a mom." I counted that as a huge compliment.

Their votes of approval made me think I'd done something right. It's been said that "the proof of the pudding is in the eating." They are my pudding.

I began writing this book after Jason and Jodi both graduated from college and started their own careers. I still remember Jodi's favorite line as we struggled through the teen years together: "Mom, don't worry; this will provide material for another chapter of your book." She'd be so disappointed if I didn't follow through!

7. I feel certain my tips for raising children have merit.

Before I started to write, I decided I'd better first share my ideas with others and see if they worked. So I taught a four-week workshop on parenting. It was suggested that both husbands and wives attend, but the class ran during the same hours as Monday-night football. That first week a few wives attended alone while the game raged on at home, but the second week every husband came along. To my delight, they asked me to extend the course, but my calendar was full. Six months later one of the *husbands* called and invited me to present a six-week series to their young parents Bible study group. Seven couples participated and during that time saw changed behavior in their children as they changed their parenting approaches.

8. I kept telling people I was writing a book.
If I didn't finish this book, everyone would think I was lying. It would be embarrassing to have this carved on my tombstone: "She had a book in progress."

9. I owe it to my mom, husband, and kids.
Mom taught me useful tips about raising infants that got my children off to a good start (maybe those tips will be in my next book). She knew about positive reinforcement and behavior modification before they had a name for it.

Barry hung in there with me all the way, even though he was a stepdad. He never turned away or tried to put ownership off on me. We parented as a team, with God's help.

The final stamp of approval will have to come from Jason and Jodi. Their lives were my "test case," and I haven't changed their names to protect the innocent!

10. I need a book.
My work has been published in magazines, such as *Decision, Clubhouse, Southwest Art, Western Horseman, Joyful Woman, Quilt World, American Iron, Power for Living, Our Family, Electronic Learning, Good Old Days, Toastmaster,* and many others. But magazines appear on the newsstand for a month and then are gone.

When I accept a speaking engagement, the contact person always asks, "What do you write?" I explain that I freelance for magazines, then name a few. They are unimpressed and ask, "Yes, but have you written a book?"

Well, now I have, and this is it.

CHAPTER ONE

Good Morning!

Some children bounce out of bed, ready to meet the world with a smile. Others slither out, hoping to be left alone until the glare of the bathroom light becomes bearable or until the snapping of the cereal has ceased. Respect that difference, as long as they are up and moving.

I'm partial to a slow start, so I like to ease into morning conversation, testing the waters carefully, and then wading in cautiously. If you start out with nagging, whining, or ordering, the whole crew may organize a mutiny, and you have sabotaged your own ship. We are all different, so take it easy.

I can remember my father hammering out a cadence on my door and singing the words to his favorite World War II song, "Oh, How I Hate to Get Up in the Morning." It was an irritating sound, but better than an alarm clock—more of a personal touch. I knew he was there and that he cared about my sister and me getting up and getting ready for school. It was his idea of a cheerful sound. About the same time, the aroma of toast and eggs would make its way to our room. Mom was always a step ahead, preparing breakfast, and seeing us off in a good mood before she went to work.

A cheerful "Good morning" (not too loud) sets the mood for the day. It is polite and positive. The conversation and activity that follow depend on individual needs.

At our house, when the children were growing up, we expected a simple greeting from everyone. Acknowledging one another's presence adds to the security of the home. Maybe a pat on the behind or a hug, if that suits the receiver. Jodi's greeting sometimes dwindled to a simple wave of the hand as she stumbled out of her bedroom. Jason often settled on a handshake, accompanied by a weak smile. Both counted as greetings in my book, and we were off to a good start.

Ample sleep, of course, is the first prerequisite to a good morning get-up. You will find tips on how to determine your child's sleeping requirements discussed in chapter 29, "Now I Lay Me Down to Sleep."

Try this: Greet your child with words that are uplifting. "Good morning, Sunshine" may be enough. But remember, the first thing you say sets the tone for the whole morning.

"Joy cometh in the morning." Psalm 30:5.

CHAPTER TWO

Whose Turn in the Bathroom?

Choreographing the use of the bathroom can be tricky but not impossible. Back in the "good ole days" one bathroom per dwelling was common. (How did we ever manage?) The little house I grew up in had two bedrooms and one bathroom with only a tub. Of course, all the same gender could share the facilities. There were times when we three women had the mirror, toilet, and tub in simultaneous use. Poor Dad was out of luck.

My mother helped each of us wash our hair in the kitchen sink. We didn't have electrical paraphernalia like blow dryers, curling irons, and electrolysis machines. Nowadays a high-tech bathroom can be hazardous and result in electrical and cosmetic disaster.

Our son and daughter worked out their own plan. Their bathroom was never empty, but they moved back and forth smoothly throughout the various stages of readiness. One might catch a glimpse of a towel-draped body darting across the hall to a bedroom as the other shot into the bathroom for the next step of the routine.

Some hairdos are impossible to create in a steamy bath-

Raising Kids Right

room, and there are other activities that call for some private time. The kids found it possible to share the last phase of hairstyling, as long as Jodi didn't misdirect the hair spray and Jason didn't hog the mirror.

The plan included a shower time allowance of seven minutes, imposed by Barry to avoid problems with the septic tank. He used me as the test case to come up with the time allotment. I could shower, wash my hair, and shave my legs in that amount of time. Nobody had more than that to accomplish, so that became the standard. In order to stick to the time frame, Jason and Jodi had to get started promptly. They became more punctual while learning to share and compromise.

Each time one party changed his/her activities, it required reworking the whole schedule. The kids used the same routine for the nine years they were in elementary school. They instituted changes when Jason started high school, and again when Jodi joined him there.

Occasionally the system would break down because someone overslept, abused the time limits, or nature called and an immediate response was crucial. Then thumping on the wall, banging on the door, and angry words would beat out the cadence of a morning gone sour. Learning to share a bathroom is like training for marriage. Someday they will be sharing with spouses, and banging on the door will not be appropriate behavior.

Barry and I decided to take our own advice. For years we had argued over our individual use of the toothpaste and sink. Our bathroom had two sinks, but we both used the one by the medicine cabinet (force of habit, I guess). After taking a better look, I solved the problem by buying two tubes of toothpaste and moving over to the other sink. Sometimes the solution is incredibly simple if we will stop and look at the problem unemotionally.

Whose Turn in the Bathroom?

Try this: Those who share each bathroom need to make a plan, working out every logistical detail. Their plan will include starting times and procedure. Consider storage areas for grooming supplies, as well as who will hang his/her towels where. It's a good lesson in cooperation.

(The importance of cleanliness is discussed later in chapter 12, "Did You Wash Behind Your Ears?")

"Do not merely look out for your own personal interests, but also for the interests of others." Philippians 2:4, NASB.

CHAPTER THREE

I Don't Have a Thing to Wear

One day at the mall I found myself standing in line behind a girl of about 12. Her fair skin and blond roots told me her jet-black hair was dyed. She had a ring in her nose and several down the sides of each ear. Her jeans hung off her hips, exposing her tummy under a skin tight midriff knit top. I wanted to reach out, hug her, and say, "Who forgot to love you? How dare they?" Her whole get-up screamed, "What more can I do to get someone's attention?"

As the parent, you select your preschool children's clothing. When they start school, you begin to see the first signs of peer pressure. They want to dress like others, and you will find it harder and harder to deny their desires, but you can direct their choices.

Laying out clothes the night before cuts down on morning problems. The child can take an active part in the selection of outfits, and this practice is a good lesson in decision-making. It also alleviates running around at the last minute looking for a lost shoe or the blouse someone planned to wear that is crumpled up in the dryer.

It's easier to set standards of dress that are acceptable

I Don't Have a Thing to Wear

before going shopping. At the store, supervision and agreement is important. If you don't bring unacceptable clothing home from the store, you won't have to argue about it later. By then it is not only too late, but often horrifying to wait for impromptu creations that appear from the bedroom at the last minute.

Jason wore corduroy pants and plaid shirts from age 7 until he was halfway through college. He looked presentable and felt comfortable, so why worry? I was lucky he was so easy to please. When he was going through the rapid growing periods, it was the early seventies. Stores were selling pants with sections of colorful materials (hippie-style bell bottoms). When Jason's pant legs got too short, I would cut them off at the knees, add an extension of denim or other fabric, and then sew the leg back on. Considered rather "cool" at the time, the technique extended the life of his pants by a few months. Most boys wear out the knees before the zipper really starts working smoothly. But Jason was as conservative about his physical activity as he was about his mode of dress.

Jodi, on the other hand, loved to be just a little different. We always called her our "trendsetter." No one was too eager to follow her lead, though. She didn't emulate the rock stars or the magazine ads, but liked to dream up her own combinations. One day she came into the living room dressed in her grandfather's mustard-yellow bowling shirt and lime-green bike shorts. Most of her outfits were acceptable, but that one won her a free trip back to her bedroom to try again.

I remember a student who was quite overweight. She wore brightly colored solids that stretched tightly across the rolls of her midriff and newly developing breasts. The seams of her polyester pants cried out for mercy. She was

Raising Kids Right

so much larger than all the other girls, she just didn't fit in—with the class or her clothes.

One day I asked her to stay after class. I told her about a friend of mine who had a large frame. The way my friend dressed herself and carried her body made her quite striking. She made sure her clothes fit perfectly or were stylishly oversized, but she never let herself look like she'd been poured into her outfit.

I gave the girl an opportunity to talk about what clothes might be more flattering to her particular figure. My purpose was to help her make choices that would complement her build, but I worried all night that I might have offended her.

The next day she came to school dressed in loose-fitting clothing and looked like someone who had taken time to care about herself. She also looked more comfortable. I made sure to tell her what a good choice she had made. From then on she came into class with a look in her eye that seemed to say "How am I doing?" My guess is that she received negative responses from those she loved. It was my job to fill those wounds with positive praise.

I hope she always remembers to take the time to do the best she can with what she has. If we don't affirm children in a positive way for positive choices, they will find other ways to get our attention.

When you send your children off to school, consider three questions:
1. Is the outfit suitable for the classroom?
2. Is the outfit suitable for the activities of the day?
3. Is the outfit suitable for today's weather?

Suitable for the classroom

What is suitable for the classroom? This varies drasti-

I Don't Have a Thing to Wear

cally, depending on where you live. In California and Arizona, for example, it's not unusual to have air-conditioned classrooms. When activity is minimal and students are doing mental work, they don't generate much heat. Their circulation slows down, and a sweater may be necessary. When the outside temperatures rise above 90, they'll be glad to shed the sweater and romp in lightweight attire.

In areas where the winters are freezing, no one wears the same clothing outside as inside. Coming inside means shedding heavy outer layers.

The important thing to remember is that the child who is physically uncomfortable inside will not have maximum opportunity to learn. When your child becomes too warm or too cold, his/her attention leaves the learning process and centers on the more basic need for comfort.

Suitable for the activities of the day

A suitable outfit for school should not distract others or violate the dress code of the school. It should also be adaptable to both inside and outside activities.

In most schools, students must wear tennis shoes or soft-closed shoes for physical education activities. Most schools won't allow students to participate without the correct type of footwear. When you send children to school without proper clothing or footwear for outdoor sports, it affects his grade. They also lose a chance to tone their bodies and learn athletic skills. Inexpensive tennis shoes are available in most supermarkets—they don't have to be stylish, just functional.

What other activities has the teacher planned? Will the class be performing on the stage where they need to dress consistently or in a certain color? Will your daughter be turning flips on the monkey bars where shorts worn under

Raising Kids Right

a skirt would preserve her modesty? Will your son be kneeling in the wet grass while playing football?

Suitable for today's weather

If you live in an area where the weather is likely to change quickly, help your child go to school prepared for changes. I see children come to school without jackets on rainy or windy days and wonder, "Where was the parent when that child left home?"

It took me a long time to realize that each child's personal thermostat is unique. Jodi was "warm-blooded." I'm "cold-blooded." I would send her to nursery school with an undershirt, blouse, and pinafore. When her dad picked her up in the afternoon, she'd appear with the blouse and undershirt over her arm. This frustrated me, and it continued right into kindergarten. Finally I decided it was better to dress her in a cool outfit with a sweater or jacket she could shed than to force her into a striptease act. Layering clothes can add flexibility. The child who tends to be warm-blooded can take off a layer, while the cold-blooded shiverer can add a layer.

Improper dress can restrict your child's chances to participate and make him/her feel "different." Don't be conned into thinking that your child has to have every designer fashion that is "in," but do be sensitive to what is acceptable. Let your child know it's OK to be an individual and not necessary to do what everyone else is doing.

It is our responsibility to assist our children in making good choices until they are capable of making good choices alone. Making choices together accomplishes other important objectives. It gives you a picture of what your child is doing at school, and lets your child know that you care, even when he/she is at school. It gives a child a secure feeling to know someone cares.

I Don't Have a Thing to Wear

Remember, someday you won't be there to help anymore. How well prepared is your child to think through facts and formulate decisions? You are teaching problem-solving and decision-making at an early age. As an adult, his/her decisions will warm your heart rather than break it.

Try this: Lay out clothes at bedtime. Before your child leaves for school, ask if he/she will be prepared should the weather get colder or warmer. Are there any special sports or dramatic events requiring a change of clothing? Let him/her take part in the planning.

"Train up a child in the way he should go: and when he is old, he will not depart from it." Proverbs 22:6.

CHAPTER FOUR

What's for Breakfast?

My mother always said, "Eat breakfast fit for a king, lunch fit for a prince, and dinner fit for a pauper." We need the most fuel during our productive hours and the least when we go to sleep.

A child needs nourishment to meet the demands of the day. Having a satisfied stomach fulfills a basic need. When the basic need for food is not met, a child's behavior may be severely affected. The stomach that rumbles and cries out for food can be quite distracting. Some children become extremely nervous and display almost uncontrollable behavior, twitching, wiggling, and bouncing. Others become lethargic and have trouble concentrating. In either case, the child's concern is not on learning. Whether consciously or unconsciously, he/she craves nourishment.

Some parents adhere to the belief that children need to eat in the morning, but place no importance on *what* they eat. Bizarre behavior can also result from an *improper* breakfast. Sometimes the wrong breakfast is as bad as no breakfast at all. Students who have eaten cookies, doughnuts, heavily sugared cereal, or syrupy pancakes often display a variety of

What's for Breakfast?

strange behaviors, similar to children who come to school hungry. It depends on the child's chemical makeup.

Like cars, we humans also need fuel at regular intervals. Eating the right food at the right time helps keep blood sugar level and energy constant. And like cars, some of us run richer than others and need higher octane, but we still need the right fuel.

When a student is unable to concentrate in class, I have two pat questions I ask: "What time did you go to bed last night?" and "What did you eat for breakfast?" Therein usually lies the answer to the problem.

If you have time to fix breakfast, prepare eggs, toast, bagels, or cereal with little or no sugar. Fruit is always good.

If your school offers a nutrition break or snack time for the students, send a snack that is vitamin rich and sugar and fat poor, such as bread, fruit, crackers, and vegetables. You and your children could make up a list of foods that they would eat and enjoy. Again, you are allowing them to take part in decision making while you save money.

As a mother, I cringed at the amount of food my children wasted until I started letting them help plan their lunches and snacks. No use putting in expensive food that they give away or throw away. I hate to think of the millions of starving people in the world while the garbage cans at school are overflowing with food that mothers sent but junior didn't like.

Back to the subject of sugar. There have been times when I've rewarded my whole class with one piece of candy each. The results were horrendous. Moments later I was peeling them off the walls.

To many, sugar is a "fix," the same as drugs are to an addict. The effect is an extreme high energy that is short-lived, followed by a letdown. It puts the body in a turmoil of rapid

Raising Kids Right

physiological change that is not conducive to learning.

For more than 30 years I've observed the results of poor nutrition in classes. Each year fewer and fewer children come to school with proper breakfasts under their belts. The most common reason is that both parents work outside the home and nobody has time to fix breakfast.

Don't get me wrong. I was also a working mother from the time my children were babies. The only time my kids got pancakes, eggs, waffles, and French toast was for the evening meal, occasionally. Imagine their surprise when they saw their first breakfast menu and those items were on it!

My brother-in-law's favorite breakfast is a plateful of last night's dinner warmed in the microwave. Yuck! Breakfast for dinner doesn't bother me, but the thought of dinner for breakfast makes me gag. A warmed-up dinner, however, is still better fuel than doughnuts.

Jason and Jodi learned to fix their own cereal at a very early age. If you can't handle cooking in the morning, teach your children some good eating habits and provide the food they can prepare. With encouragement, they will learn fast.

The few extra moments it takes to eat breakfast will increase your children's productivity. They will feel better and think better. Sitting down to the meal together nourishes them in yet another way, building security and belonging. All parents want their children to succeed. Give them the best preparation by sending them to school nutritionally satisfied. After all, you won't see them all day long, and they need fuel to perform at maximum capacity.

Recently I made several visits to a wonderful nutritionist who taught me how to eat. For years I believed that eating between meals was a crime. Now I learn that eating a little snack every two hours or so is a much better sys-

What's for Breakfast?

tem—especially if the food is low in fat, sugar, preservatives, and cholesterol.

When you put gas in your car, you don't buy gas that you know would damage the engine. It's also not recommended to fill a tank with gas and then run it until it is out of fuel completely. When that happens, it leads to all kinds of other problems. Hence, it is customary to keep some gas in a car at all times. The human body also needs fuel and shouldn't be run on empty before refueling. The tank doesn't have to be full, just fueled.

Try this: If making breakfast is a hardship because of busy schedules, here's a recipe anyone can make. It fills nutritional needs and gives your child energy to go on.

In the blender:
> ½ to ¾ cup milk (low-fat or nonfat is probably best)
> ½ cup fresh fruit (banana, strawberries, peaches, cherries, pears, oranges, etc.)

Blend and drink.

I've been giving this recipe to children for years. Those who are allowed to use the blender can prepare it themselves. They can have fun creating new ideas I haven't thought of.

"Eat only what you need." Proverbs 25:16, NASB.

CHAPTER FIVE

What's on TV?

It is not unusual for an American family to start their morning to the blare of a TV. They become so accustomed to the noise they can't get along without it. We were one of those families. The effects were subtle at first, but became more and more damaging. With the TV on, progress slowed, the noise level went up, and tension rose among the troops.

There is no reason for children to watch TV in the morning unless they have eaten breakfast, gotten dressed, completed homework, finished chores, prepared lunch, and stacked up all materials destined for school. If *all* of this is accomplished, then some TV might be a great reward for a job well done!

The year Jason started kindergarten, I became frustrated by seeing him parked in front of the TV in his pajamas when it was time to go to school. I would stack his clothes beside him as he sat mesmerized and remind him over and over that I would be leaving soon. I taught fourth grade at the same country school where Jason attended kindergarten, so of course we rode to school together. The prob-

What's on TV?

lem was that he was causing me to be late every morning. Finally I decided he would never learn responsibility if I kept nagging.

We had a little talk. (I think I did all the talking.) It went something like this: "From now on, I'm leaving for work at five minutes to 8:00. I won't be nagging you anymore. If you are ready on time, we'll go to school together. If you aren't, you will have to walk to school." (Fortunately, it was only four blocks.)

The next day, when it was time to leave, I said, "Goodbye, Jason; I'll see you at school," and headed out the door. Jason jumped to his feet. He grabbed his clean clothes and followed me to the car, still clad in his PJs. He was crying, but he began to dress himself as fast as he could. It didn't take long to drive four blocks, and he wiggled into his pants just as I parked the car. I marched away toward the campus as he was lacing his shoes. He may have been hating me for that brief moment, but he got the message. I didn't look back because I had to stay firm, and I didn't want him to see the tears in my eyes.

It was hard for me to carry through, but I never had to wait on him again. We did away with morning TV unless he was ready to go. Jason became the one in the family who planned enough time to get ready and was usually punctual. He never wanted to get caught with his pants down again.

He also learned that he could trust me to do what I said I would do. The reason parents get into the habit of nagging is they don't intend to follow through and the child knows it. The responsibility hasn't been given to the child, and he/she knows that too.

Try this: Keep the TV off in the mornings unless *everything*

Raising Kids Right

is finished. Your home will be quieter and calmer in the morning. There will be time for family conversation about everyone's schedule and the expectations of the day.

"Remember how short my time is." Psalm 89:47.

CHAPTER SIX

Clean Up Your Room

How important is it to leave each room in order? Sometimes when I leave for work, my room isn't perfect. A bolt of lightning has never struck me down yet, although I've been expecting it. It's not worth ruining your whole day over.

The problem is that small amounts of clutter accumulate, and soon you can't wade through the kids' rooms without fear of great bodily injury. Out of necessity, the job must get done.

I tried various methods. When Jason was about 3, I made a checklist. I listed the chores I expected him to do on a daily basis. If the chores were completed, I put a star on the chart. To reward him for repeated success, I read him a story, played a game, or took a walk with him. We both benefited.

If the chore wasn't completed, I cut out TV for the evening, or some other privilege. Jason would fill up the chart with stars and ask to have other chores added to the chart. I was consistent, so he was too.

Unfortunately, my consistency must have been worn

Raising Kids Right

out when Jodi came along. We called Jodi our "finder." She found things everywhere. And when she found them, she kept them in her room. She had collections of match books, stuffed toys, business cards, keys, place mats, doodads, thingamajigs, and whatchamacallits. One can was full of nuts, bolts, and whatever else falls off a car when it goes around the corner that she collected by our roadside. Cleaning her room was impossible.

I was working all day, and then working all night cleaning house. So I hired a housekeeper to come once a week. At first I had a college girl, and then I hired a high school boy. He cleaned as well as any woman I ever had, and was willing to work for less than an adult. When he quit, I hired a woman who stuck with us for 17 years. She became like a patsy for the kids and a best friend to me. Whenever something was lost or broken, Jason and Jodi replied in unison, "Virginia did it!" Virginia insisted that she was worth the price, just so we had someone to blame things on and keep peace in the family.

A housekeeper can be an expensive luxury, but there are ways to have one for less. Virginia washed all her clothes at my house while she was washing ours. She used our water, soap, and electricity. We sorted and saved recyclable materials for her, gave her clothing, took her swimming, and lots more to compensate for a mediocre wage. In spite of all that, she still screamed, "Hazardous duty pay!" whenever she entered Jodi's room. When Jodi's room got so bad I couldn't stand it, my last ditch effort was to say "You are not leaving the house until your room is cleaned up."

I feel like a failure in the area of teaching children to clean their rooms. Jodi came back home and lived for two years between earning her B.S. and going back for her master's degree. We loved having her home and gladly wel-

Clean Up Your Room

comed her back, but her room environment was still an issue. In order to live peacefully, I charged her $150 per month with one interesting twist. For every day her room was clean, she would get back $5. So if the room was cleaned up every day, she got free rent. That worked great for about four months. Then Jodi started planning for a trip to Texas. Piles of clothes began to collect in preparation for her packing. I let it go, because packing is expected to be messy. When she returned, I let it go again because I thought it was only fair to give her a few days to unpack and get things back to normal. Unfortunately, my idea of normal and Jodi's idea have never coincided. I finally put a chart on her door, just like we used with Jason when he was a kid. And until she moved out, that did the trick.

I know I could have done better if I had remained consistent. Sometimes it just gets to be too much of an effort. If I had it to do over again, I'd assign the chore, decide on the reward or reinforcement, and state a definite consequence that would be paid if the chore was not completed. I'd make all three reasonable and stick to it like glue.

Some parents feel this is bribery. According to Webster's dictionary a bribe is a price, reward, gift, or favor bestowed or promised *with a view to pervert the judgment or corrupt the conduct of a person.*

The intent is to encourage appropriate behavior, not pervert it. After all, isn't the reward and denial system what adults respond to? For example, a job is available. The boss sets the standards of how that job is to be done and what is expected. The employee who meets the standards of proficiency is rewarded with a paycheck and, later, receives raises or benefits. The employee who can't handle the job is either demoted or fired. At any rate, he/she does not get the reward.

Raising Kids Right

If you nag children to do anything, they are *not* learning to take responsibility, even when they finally complete the chore. They are only learning that *you* never give up. When a child learns to take positive action for positive rewards, you are headed in the right direction. That is what raising kids is all about.

We all work for rewards, whether they are nonsocial, social, or spiritual. A nonsocial reward is money, food, points or some concrete thing. A social reward is a kind word, pat on the back, or public acknowledgment. A spiritual reward is gaining glory for the Lord and laying treasures up in heaven.

I must confess that as I was proofreading this chapter, Virginia walked by and added, "If all else fails, get a housekeeper!"

Try this:
1. Make expectations clear.
2. Make rewards not too big and not too small.
3. Reward on time.
4. Be consistent.
5. Keep your promises.
6. Don't nag or remind the child! Just keep the system.

"Create in me a clean heart, O God; and renew a right spirit within me. " Psalm 51:10.

CHAPTER 7:

Where Are Your Books?

"Where are your books?" "Did you get your lunch?" "Is this your gym bag?" "Wasn't your science project due today?"

It's easy to get flustered when time is growing short and you discover there are details not yet completed. One morning the car was the only thing that was ready to go as each of us beat a path back to the house to collect articles we would be needing at school that day. I certainly couldn't reprimand the children when I was guilty of the same disorganization. There is nothing more frustrating than running around at the last moment looking for coats, getting notes signed, and trying to make peanut butter and jelly sandwiches, all at the same time.

Imagine a crew of firefighters responding to an alarm, running in every direction as they try to find their turnouts, helmets, gloves, and boots. Of course that doesn't happen, because they have a place for everything. When the alarm sounds, there is no guessing game.

We decided we could do the same thing. A hutch near the back door became our "parking place" for all the items that would be going with us the next morning. Each of us had our spot. The kids were better at keeping their things organized than I was. I still have a spot where I pile the things that are going to work with me the next day. It's my car keys that I can't ever find.

If everybody at your house is running around looking for something they need at the last minute, there's a solution.

Try this: Designate a place for each family member to stack "stuff." It may be a certain chair, table, or the piano bench. When homework is completed, it is placed in that spot. When lunches are prepared, they are put in that spot. If there are any notes to the teacher, school forms, or science projects, they go there also. Coats, gloves, boots, and caps can be nearby for easy access.

"Prepared unto every good work." 2 Timothy 2:21.

CHAPTER 8:

'Bye, Kids; See You Later

As a classroom teacher, not a day goes by that I don't encounter a student who has come to school upset about something that happened at home. Yes, goodbyes are just as important as good mornings.

Ten-year-old Tommy came to school and sat against the wall in the hallway, crying. I asked if I could help.

"My mom has left us," Tommy choked out. "It's my fault. I do everything wrong. I never clean my room!"

Tommy's mother had dropped him off at school. Her parting words threatened desertion because he didn't clean up his room, and he was sure she had gone away. And this poor boy thought her departure was all his fault.

How was his day at school? Rotten. He cried, off and on, and never had his mind on the lessons. His mind was still at home, cleaning his room, or somehow making amends with Mother.

I called her during my break and found that she was recovering nicely from the outburst that had left her son devastated and feeling abandoned. She had no idea of the hurt he was feeling.

Raising Kids Right

Some children come to school with emotional wounds. If the child has been nagged all morning about being slow, forgetful, or messy, he brings that identity to school. While the teacher creates theatrical extravaganzas to motivate his learning, he is still hearing a private recording of his beloved parents saying, "You're so slow!" "Your room is a pigsty!" "You'll never get anywhere!" All this translates into "I'm a mess. I'm a failure."

What's really happened is that the parent has failed to help the child learn to take responsibility and loads the failure on the child. The child then leaves home, burdened with guilt, anxiety, and negative feelings about himself that spell failure. The teacher can stroke the child with positive words in an effort to soothe the hurting, but as a parent you have the most influence. Your attitude molds your child's identity.

Your influence on your child's self-esteem and feelings of worth is greater than you think. When parents talk *about* their children, their children are listening. When parents talk *to* their children, their children are listening. It may not seem like it sometimes, but be assured that your child can quote, verbatim, any negative or positive thing you ever said about his or her character or learning abilities. Your child will probably acquire whatever characteristics you verbally assign, because you have stated your expectations. Be kind. Let your children know how much you appreciate their behavior and encourage them to do their best.

When you say goodbye each morning, this is your last chance to program some positive data into your child before he/she goes off to school. Your child needs to hear words of love, confidence, and encouragement. Even if he/she hasn't done everything perfectly, the unconditional love of a parent or guardian can lift a child to new heights

'Bye, Kids; See You Later

of self-esteem. Your child needs to know that he/she is loved, even while making mistakes. After all, Christ loved us when we were yet sinners (Romans 5:8).

"Have a great day." "I love you." "I'm so proud of you!" These are power-packed words. Top it off with "God go with you" or "Jesus loves you." If the whole morning has been rough and disorganized, these words may undo the damage.

There will be days when things won't look so rosy. Maybe the alarm doesn't go off, the washing machine runs over, someone spills milk, and the dogs turn over all the garbage cans. Sometimes we make a mess of things and need to apologize and wipe the slate clean. It's OK to say "I'm sorry this morning was so disorganized and confused. We'll do better tomorrow. I love you."

Don't think, however, that every morning can be chaotic and filled with angry words that can be forgotten with a sweet send-off at the door. Your actions will always speak louder than words. It takes effort to make each morning an improvement over the previous one.

When my children were particularly concerned about a test or a situation at school, we would share a quick prayer together and put God in charge. That's the way it should be anyway.

Try this: Make your morning farewell a positive one. Let your children know of your love and support. A hug, a kiss, and loving words of encouragement will bridge the gap between home and school. They will take with them the confidence that you are, at home or work, caring about them and rooting for their success.

"If God be for us, who can be against us?" Romans 8:31.

CHAPTER NINE

Don't Be Late!

No matter how your children get to school, they need to be on time. When they arrive late, they are put in the position of trying to explain to the attendance clerk, and no matter what the child says, the clerk is thinking you are responsible.

"Mom didn't wake up on time." "Dad forgot his briefcase at home, and we had to go back."

The clerk issues a tardy slip, and your child goes to class late. The teacher has already taken roll and started the morning activities. Regardless of what the tardy slip says, the teacher is wishing the student hadn't missed the openers. Now all the children will have to wait while he/she makes changes in the attendance record; they are distracted, and the routine is interrupted. Everyone wishes your child had been there on time so they wouldn't have to keep backing up to get started again.

Getting your child to school on time is more than being a good parent. It's modeling a good work ethic, getting your child to the starting line even with all the other kids.

When your child is absent from school, it is imperative

that you send a note to school upon his/her return to class. In the public school system that note is very important—it is what allows the district to get paid from the state. Any day that is unaccounted for is unpaid. Even in a private school, that note is very important for recordkeeping purposes. Think of it as a ticket back to class, and be specific about the reason for the absence. It's better for you to explain than to put your child on the spot with the attendance clerk.

Important experiences happen for your child at school. It was always an exciting time when one of our kids got to be student of the week or made some sort of special presentation. Jodi still remembers getting to take her Cookie Monster puppet to school to share with her second-grade class. Her teacher liked the puppet so much that he asked Jodi to bring it in on other occasions to use for other lessons. She was delighted with that special interest he took.

Some teachers let the student of the week create a little display of pictures, momentos, and valued artifacts. Get involved in that activity so your child will enjoy that week of fame. It doesn't have to be bigger and better—it just has to be special.

Try this: Get your children to school on time. Automatically write a note and send it to school with them after every absence. Help your child enjoy special school events by taking part in his/her celebration.

"The Lord thy God hath chosen thee to be a special people." Deuteronomy 7:6.

CHAPTER TEN

An Apple for the Teacher?

Think back to the best teacher you ever had. The qualities he/she displayed were probably just right for your learning style. If you were an auditory learner, the teacher you liked best probably told great stories. If you were a visual learner, your favorite teacher probably showed movies and produced great visual aids for you to look at. Kinesthetic learners like to handle materials, build, create, and get right in the middle of things. If you were one of those, you probably remember building a mission, a hogan, or reenacting the Battle of Bull Run.

There are as many different learning styles as there are teaching strategies. It is as hard to generalize about teachers as it is to generalize about students. Each one is an individual.

If your children go to school with respect for the teacher, their chances for success are heightened. Their willingness to cooperate and accept the teacher as the authority in the classroom puts aside barriers that impede learning.

In an age when lawsuits abound, we find more and

An Apple for the Teacher?

more students coming to school with the attitude that the teacher better not breathe wrong or the parents will sue. It's a frame of mind that comes from home.

In the old days students knew that if they got in trouble at school, they would also be in trouble at home. Now teachers often finds themselves powerless at school, and with little support from the parents. Some parents are so busy with their jobs that they have little time to respond to a teacher's notes or calls.

In most cases, the teacher has the best interest of the children in mind. That doesn't mean he/she will never make a mistake or fall short of your expectations.

An irate parent once called me at home. "The assignment you gave my child was unreasonable!" he shouted.

I had asked the children to make a freehand drawing of a map of the United States. It was nothing to get so excited about. I figured I probably gave about 900 assignments in a year. In my 23 years of teaching, that's more than 20,000 assignments and 500,000 individual papers to correct. If one assignment was unreasonable, my average wasn't too bad.

The Bible states in James 3:1, "Let not many of you become teachers, my brethren, knowing that as such we shall incur a stricter judgment" (NASB). Teachers are judged more harshly, it's true. It's up to the parents to instill respect for the teacher as an authority figure. Then expect the best from the teacher and from your children.

If you become unhappy with the teacher, make an appointment to meet with him/her. If the situation doesn't become better, give the teacher a second chance. You would want the teacher to give your child a second chance. If you are still not satisfied, follow the correct procedure and make an appointment to talk with the principal.

It's easy to get emotional when a problem involves your

children. It is normal to want to protect them. Don't take sides, however, until you have heard *both* sides. If attacked, the teacher may become defensive. He/she is protecting his/her career and livelihood.

In the teaching profession, if a person is fired it usually means instant death to that career. So approach the teacher with the desire to work out a mutually agreeable solution, and he/she will be delighted to work with you. Remember, the teacher has 25 to 35 children like yours, some worse and some better, with all of their differences and difficulties with which to struggle. Some have learning disabilities, and others come to school emotionally or socially bankrupt. Many children need first aid for their bleeding hearts. Have mercy on the teacher and give him/her the benefit of the doubt.

Almost all newspaper or magazine articles about teachers or schools these days are negative. They usually sensationalize an offense of one lone teacher or the failures of individual students who decided too late that there was a purpose for school, or exaggerate test scores that have little validity in predicting success. Do what you can to improve the image of the person who is taking responsibility for your child all day long.

You may find that you disagree with curriculum or with the personal beliefs of the teacher. It is always important to stay as involved as possible. Use these opportunities to talk to your children about your beliefs and back them up with Scripture. If your child is grounded in the Word, he/she will be ready for the future. School is only the first place children will find conflicting beliefs, morals, and behavior standards. You can pave the way to a good relationship between your child and his teacher.

I made a terrible mistake before my Jodi started school. One day in the teachers' workroom I jokingly said to the kindergarten teacher, "I sure hope I can retire before Jodi

An Apple for the Teacher?

gets to the fourth grade." I taught fourth grade at the time, and the school was so small it was inevitable that she would be in my class. I implied Jodi was a discipline problem that I didn't care to handle. Because of that chance remark, the kindergarten teacher was waiting for Jodi and anticipating problems. I had labeled my child and set her up without even realizing it. Kindergarten was not a good year for Jodi, and my heart ached for her. She was treated unfairly, and the more I tried to "fix" it, the worse it got.

The following fall I saw the first grade teacher preparing for school. "Hi, Edith. Jodi is sure excited about going to the first grade. Her brother has been telling her about you, and she can hardly wait to be in your class."

Edith beamed and asked if Jodi would like to come help her set up the classroom before school started. I had only told the truth, but again I had set Jodi up. This time the teacher was looking forward to a first grader who was excited about school and eager to have her for a teacher. Jodi had a wonderful year in the first grade and loved Mrs. Lambert. Though she retired long ago, she still writes to me to ask about Jodi and her progress in life.

Try this: Think of the teacher as a friend, and take time to get acquainted at the beginning of the year. Send a note once in a while and let the teacher know how much you appreciate what he/she is doing for your child. You have no idea how seldom teachers receive any positive feedback.

Fill your child with positive ideas about the teacher. It's OK to mention some of your child's talents to the teacher so he/she can be looking for those strengths. You can help create a positive atmosphere of cooperation and respect.

"A word fitly spoken is like apples of gold in pictures of silver." Proverbs 25:11.

CHAPTER ELEVEN

How Can I Help?

There is a certain amount of guilt that goes along with being a working parent. We put it on ourselves, and we hear it from others, but our children can lay a trip on us with the simplest remark.

When Jason was in the fourth grade (which means I was his teacher), he said, "I wish you were at home with cookies and milk when I got home, like other mothers." I felt the sting. I thought, *I'm not like other mothers. I've let them down. There is an empty spot in his life where a mother is supposed to be.*

I took the next two days off for personal leave. The first day both kids jumped off the bus and ran to the house for their cookies and milk. What fun!

"Missed you at school today, Mom," Jason said over his shoulder as he slipped out the door. Then he was on his bike and headed for his friend's house to play.

Jodi went in her room to play with her Barbi dolls and seemed happy to be home so early. The next day she called me from school to ask if she could ride the bus home with a friend and could I pick her up at 5:00. "Oh, and Mom,

How Can I Help?

Jason said he'll be playing at Shane's house and could you pick him up, too?"

So there I sat, alone, with my cookies and milk. I felt more worthless than ever. They really didn't mean they wanted me there every day, but once was fine. I wondered if they were just testing me. Whatever, I think the two days off taught us all something. They learned that arriving home early to cookies and milk wasn't exactly what they thought it would be, and I learned that once in a while it pays to let them know I'd do anything for them.

I said all that to say this. Since you can't be waiting at home with cookies and milk every day, find ways to be involved in their school life so they know you care. Let's face it, even if you are a Mr. Mom or a stay-at-home-Mom you still wouldn't be in the classroom with your children all day. Yes, you'd have the freedom to volunteer in classrooms and attend every special event. But children need to go to school of some sort. Think of your children as being at work from 8:00 to 3:00 every day from first grade through high school. Meanwhile, be as involved as you can be. Make those hours count for you and for them, either by volunteering in the classroom, working for the dollars to help support the family, or completing household chores so you can spend quality time together when the kids are home. Some parents do a combination of the three.

Get to know the teacher. Ask to see your child's school papers every day and take an interest in every subject. There are a couple questions that will get you nowhere. "How was school?" usually gets the "Fine" reply. "What did you do today?" is followed by "Nothing." As a teacher I used to review what we had learned each day before the children left school so they could answer that question intelligently.

Ask questions such as "What kind of problems did you

Raising Kids Right

solve in math today?" "How did you participate in class?" "Why do you think the teacher gave you an A on this paper?" That's a great one, because the child gets to reinforce his/her own success.

Look at the textbooks and ask questions about the pictures. If you are up on the lessons, you may be able to relate real-life experiences to what is being taught in school.

Encourage your child to bring home all notices from the teacher. These are a great source of information and keep you abreast of what's going on, even if you can't be there. Many employers will allow their workers to take special days to visit their children's school for conferences and special events. There are even ways of being there without being there. Here's how:

Try this:
Send Dad, Grandma, or a special family friend.

Ask another parent to tape the event to watch with your child later.

Send a note in the lunch box saying "I'm praying for your presentation today" or "God bless you during your test."

Remember to ask how things went, and show a sincere interest.

"Walk in wisdom . . . , redeeming the time." Colossians 4:5.

CHAPTER TWELVE

Did You Wash Behind Your Ears?

It's natural to be drawn to a person who is "squeaky clean" and fresh smelling. Adolescent children are developing an "air" of their own that must be held in check. A daily shower or bath is absolutely necessary. Deodorant, antiperspirant, powder, and other body fresheners can also add to keeping that fresh fragrance.

Unfortunately, many parents think that a child who hasn't reached adolescence doesn't have to worry about offending others. Give me a break! A classroom full of sweaty little 10-year-olds smells like wet dirt.

I thought about putting this chapter after "Whose Turn in the Bathroom?" or before "Now I Lay Me Down to Sleep." Showers usually occur during those time slots, but I wanted to talk about how being clean affects a child's acceptance at school.

During my teaching years I taught some classes in the physical education program. When an extra player was needed, I filled in. The grimy little hands that were extended to me made me cringe—not the hands, but the grime. When we were finished, my hands smelled just like theirs. I always beat a path to the washbasin.

The sad part is that other children will refuse those grimy hands and say, "Oh, yuck!" The child who comes to school dirty or stinky is avoided. Others refuse to be his/her partner, and often the child is absolutely unaware of the root of his/her unpopularity.

I could often tell which girls in my class were going to be starting their periods because of the strong, sickening-sweet odor from their unbathed bodies. At any age, children really need to bathe daily. We talked about hygiene in class, but it was still necessary to remind individuals to be more diligent about bathing.

Some children would insist they bathed daily, but telltale patterns of muddy rivulets streaking down dirty forearms and ankles were a dead giveaway. Just a little rubbing would have produced substantial dirt balls. Unsupervised bathing is often devoid of the basic necessities: hot water, soap, and a washcloth.

Try this: Teach your children that a daily shower or bath is as normal and necessary as eating. Make it part of the routine. They will have a better chance of attracting friends and feeling good about themselves at the same time. Make sure hair is brushed and nails are clean.

While you're at it, include brushing the teeth in the routine—at least before they leave the house in the morning and before bed at night. Not only is it healthy, it will save you hundreds of dollars on future dental bills.

Being clean and fresh increases a feeling of wellness. It says "I care about myself." It also increases the chances that others will care too.

"Except they wash, they eat not." Mark 7:4.

CHAPTER THIRTEEN

What's for Lunch?

I lived on peanut butter and jelly sandwiches from the first grade until fifth grade, when our elementary school built a cafeteria. I was so thrilled to have a hot lunch that I didn't care what it was. Sloppy joes, transparent gravy over instant potatoes, Jell-O, and canned green beans suited me just fine. I never went without lunch, and my mother's worrying about the starving masses in China kept me from throwing anything away.

As a teacher, I was appalled at the mounds of food thrown in the garbage. Most of the time it was because the children hadn't played any part in planning their own menu. My children weren't crazy about cafeteria food, so they opted to make their lunches when they got old enough. It was my responsibility to provide lunch money or the makings for a healthy lunch.

There are many prepared foods that can be thrown into a lunch sack rather effortlessly, although most of them are full of preservatives. It's important to consider your child's dietary needs, your food budget, and preparation time.

Raising Kids Right

Try this: Sit down with your children each month and study the school's monthly menu. Let them choose and mark which days they will eat in the cafeteria. Tack the calendar up in a convenient place.

Take the children shopping for fruit, vegetables, cereal, dairy products, and protein to make balanced lunches. They can help with reading labels and choosing appropriate foods that will be less likely to end up in the garbage. Stay away from foods that are high in sugar, fat, or preservatives.

Most important, don't let your child go without lunch. He/she needs the midday fuel. It takes energy to think, play ball, chase girls/guys, and go, go, go all day.

"When they shall be hungry, they shall fret themselves." Isaiah 8:21.

CHAPTER FOURTEEN

It's a Bitter Pill to Swallow

When a child gets sick at school, it concerns everyone—the office staff, the health clerk, the teacher, and the parents. The child's welfare is utmost, but getting in touch with commuting parents, who may be as much as an hour away, creates a problem. It's important to have alternate care available for such emergencies.

My alternate care was my friend and housekeeper, Virginia. She saw the kids through colds, flu, and concussions. One day, when Jodi was a second grader, she became very sick. She was running a temperature and came to my classroom for some TLC. The secretary called Virginia, but she was nowhere to be found. So Jodi crawled into the big cardboard box I kept in the back of the classroom for silent reading and slept all afternoon. When school was over, I took her in my arms and carried her to the car. Not all parents can do that, even if they'd like to. The school office will make every effort to contact the parents and the names on the emergency list.

Sometimes it's necessary for a child to take medicine, either regularly or for a temporary condition, and it's a nui-

Raising Kids Right

sance. New laws require the parent to bring the medication to the school in the original prescription bottle, along with a note from the doctor. If the medicine is nonprescription, it must be in the original container and be accompanied by a note from the parents for permission to medicate.

In the past, a parent could tie up a few pills in a plastic bag, stick them in the lunch box, and send the child off to school. No more. Because of the dangers caused by drug abuse, human error, and carelessness, the laws governing what goes on in schools get stricter every year. Why? To protect the school employees and to protect your children. So it's a good idea to cooperate by following the rules about medications.

Try this: Find a friend or relative who will care for your children should they become ill during the school day. It won't be easy, so plan ahead! Never send your child to school sick. Double-check with school staff to make sure you have fulfilled all the requirements so there is no question about the administration of any medication your child needs to take.

"A merry heart doeth good like a medicine." Proverbs 17:22.

CHAPTER FIFTEEN

Cat Got Your Tongue?

People who communicate effectively have a better chance of being successful in life. Those who are painfully shy have such a struggle that it can be a constant obstacle to their relationships.

To force a child who is shy to speak up is not going to help. In fact, it can cause other problems that may be worse. Neither of my children were ever shy, and I'm glad. I'm not sure if it was because of anything we did, or if they just had a "talkative gene" they inherited from their mother. Some kids are just naturally more communicative, and then there are the chatterboxes who talk incessantly.

The painfully shy children are the other extreme. A happy medium is desirable—speaks when spoken to, adds to the conversation, contributes to classroom discussion, shares original ideas, and listens respectfully to others.

Speaking is a skill. Like skiing, it can be learned and refined. A skier may be satisfied to flounder aimlessly down the slopes, or may see the need to invest in some lessons and develop the skill so it is a thing of beauty.

Children are asked to make oral reports before they are

given any instruction on how to give an oral report. If a child has little opportunity to speak at home, the oral report will be horrifying. Encourage your children to make presentations for the family, just for fun. How about reciting a poem? Then you can talk about: facing the audience, holding the head up, projecting the voice, avoiding *ahs, ums,* and *you know,* making eye contact, and smiling.

When your children are asked questions, always allow them to answer for themselves. Do not speak up on their behalf, even when you see hesitation and a search for words. Give them all the time it takes. Let them learn to speak for themselves without interruption. They will realize that you have confidence in them, and will be able to hold their own in a conversation.

Try this: Include your children in daily conversation in which each family member is highlighted to report the day's events. Don't interrupt or correct. Give value to the stories by asking questions and showing interest. *Always* let your children finish their own sentence.

Teach your kids how to make introductions, express love, give greetings, offer apologies, give sincere praise, voice gracious thanks, ask for forgiveness, and deal with conflict appropriately. These are skills that can help your children communicate clearly and in a way that is pleasing and admirable. They don't just automatically know how to express themselves; they learn from your instruction and personal example. Telling them isn't enough unless you model the same behavior in your life. Use the Scriptures as your guide.

"Be thou an example of the believers, in word, in conversation." 1 Timothy 4:12.

CHAPTER SIXTEEN

You're Dismissed

School's out. This is probably the scariest part of the day for a parent. Where are your kids? Will you pick them up? Will a neighbor pick them up? Will they ride the bus? Will they be transported to a child-care center somewhere away from the school, walk to a baby-sitter's house, or take advantage of available on-campus child care?

When you enroll your children in school, you are asked to fill out an emergency card. On that card you must name at least two other people who have your permission to pick up your children in case of an emergency. I must admit that I never took those names too seriously, and I don't think I ever told my children whom I had named.

In 1991 I was assigned as district coordinator of five on-campus child-care centers. I now know the importance of those names and numbers. When a parent doesn't show up at 6:00 p.m., we want to know that those numbers are valid and that someone will come to get the child. *You* want to know that the people you have named are willing, available, and responsible. My child-care workers will not release a child to anyone who is not listed on that emergency

Raising Kids Right

card. So take those names and numbers very seriously, and keep them current.

There is nothing more frightening than discovering your child is not where you thought! I know; it happened to me.

"Jason, I have a teachers' meeting after school today. You can play at Shane's house, but meet me back at the school by 5:00."

The meeting was in a room with no windows, and we had just started Daylight Savings Time. When we emerged from the room, much later than expected, it was dark outside, and there was no Jason. I panicked. I ran from empty classroom to empty classroom, calling his name.

"Please, everyone, get your cars and help me find Jason!" I shouted. He was only a first grader, and my mind raced through one frightening scenario after another, trying to figure out the circumstances of his disappearance. I drove straight to our house, feeling certain I would find him there, but it was completely dark. Now I was becoming hysterical. The people who brought Jodi home from nursery school must have come and gone. They had instructions to drop her off at Virginia's if they didn't find us home.

I ran into the house and called Virginia, but Jodi wasn't there. Words cannot describe my emotions. I jumped back into the car and decided to drive up and down every street. On the second block I heard a shrill whistle and in my rearview mirror saw a figure running into the rays of the streetlight, waving his arms.

It was Merrill, the postmaster, a neighbor and a sweet friend. The kids were in his house with his wife, Vickie, having doughnuts. How did they get there?

"Mom, don't you remember the night you almost knocked yourself out on the refrigerator door? You told me

You're Dismissed

that if anything ever happened to you to take Jodi and go to Merrill's house." Jason knew the plan. I guess I never expected he would have to carry through with it.

As it turned out, Jason had played at his friend's house a little too long. It was getting dark, so he decided that he'd better head home instead of back to school. When he got to the house, Jodi was just arriving from nursery school with the car pool lady. Jason, in his levelheaded, take-charge, I'm-a-competent-first-grader manner, convinced the driver that Jodi was quite safe at home with him. They left her there. The house was locked, so the kids sat on the front porch waiting for Mom. When darkness fell, Jason decided that it was too cold outside for Jodi, and that maybe something had happened to Mom. Hence, he reverted to the emergency plan and took Jodi safely down the alley to Merrill's house.

The scare made us all realize that it was imperative to have a plan, know the plan, and stick to the plan.

Try this: Update your emergency card at the school and tell your child whom you have designated for emergency pickup. Then call the people you have designated, and let them know.

Always make sure that both you and your child know where he/she is expected to be immediately after school. If this is unclear, or if the routine changes, call the school during the day and make sure you get a message to him/her.

Impress the importance of communication upon your child by modeling good communication. Make an agreement that he/she will never go anywhere after school without your permission.

"Know the way by which ye must go: for ye have not passed this way heretofore." Joshua 3:4.

CHAPTER SEVENTEEN

Free Time?

Time is a valued commodity. It is never really free. It can be wasted, spent, or killed, but if you have it on your hands and don't use it wisely, one day you'll find it has slipped away.

Think about it. Kids don't usually get into trouble or get hurt when they are involved in organized, chaperoned activities. It's when they are alone or in small groups, left to their own creative devices, that mischief reigns.

The foolish or dangerous stunts I pulled as a child were never under the watchful eyes of my parents. They were formulated when two or more kids were gathered without adult supervision.

When I was about 4, I hung by my hands from the railing on our front porch. The porch was concrete, and the railing was made of a steel water pipe. (It definitely wasn't fancy, but it gave us an entrance to our fourplex apartment that once served as housing on Camp Beale Air Force Base.) I was facing toward the house, dangling to and fro, with three neighbor kids as my interested audience.

Free Time?

"Betcha can't let go and drop to the ground," one challenged.

That seemed easy enough, but had an adult been observing, the danger would have been apparent. I took the dare and released my hands. Unfortunately, my chin met the concrete porch before my feet met the ground, and I ended up at the medical center getting stitches.

Children who are left to their own devices will often contrive activities that are dangerous to themselves or others. What one child would never dream of doing alone, he/she will enthusiastically pursue with peers. Judgment isn't developed enough to consider the consequences.

A young father once told me how frustrated he was with his 3-year-old son, who was constantly getting hurt and requiring stitches. The father had an old car with a faulty trunk latch, so he propped the trunk open with a little stick. The boy, left to play in the driveway alone, attempted to climb into the trunk of the car. He hit the stick, and the trunk lid came down on the back of his head. The father was appalled at the boy's irresponsibility. I was appalled at the *father's* irresponsibility. The boy didn't have the maturity to reason, " If I do this, that will happen."

When school was dismissed, my kids knew where they were headed, and so did I. Of course, I had the advantage of teaching in the same school they attended, so I was always available. My quitting time was much later than theirs, but at least I was available.

When school is dismissed, is there a plan for your child? Is there adult supervision? What are some of the options? Anything is better than leaving children home alone.

Here are a few ways to fill your child's time constructively:

1. After school sports. Some schools offer intramural

Raising Kids Right

sports during the school day and intermural sports after school hours. Under teachers' supervision, children are taught performance skills, as well as team spirit, integrity, confidence, responsibility, and self-control.

The Murrieta school was so small it took every willing athlete from fourth grade to eighth grade to make a team. Jason played center for the football team when he was only in the fourth grade. Once, when the team went to another school to play, the nose tackle on the opposing team was three years older than Jason and at least three times bigger. As Jason readied himself to hike the ball, the defensive man went into a three-point stance. I wanted to cover my eyes, and Jason probably did too. The tackle took one look at little Jason and said, "Don't worry, kid; I won't hurt you."

2. Music lessons. Not every child will grow up to be a great musician, but offering the opportunity to learn how to read music is a way of opening the door. Just learning the basic musical terms and notes gives a child the chance to understand how music works. Most elementary schools offer lessons in band instruments, while private lessons are available for piano and some of the orchestral instruments.

My mother insisted I learn to play the piano well enough to play for church. I have never regretted learning about music. My only regret is that I didn't practice harder, longer, and with greater enthusiasm when I had the time.

My own children both took piano lessons with even less enthusiasm than I had. Jason wanted to be a drummer, so we bought him a used drum set. That may not have been the smartest thing we ever did, because we lived in a mobile home at the time, and his practicing was a major annoyance. But we were willing to sacrifice to see him get into the elementary school band. If he wasn't beating on the drums, he was tapping on the counters or thumping on his chest.

Free Time?

One Saturday Barry was roping in a rodeo, so the kids and I were there to cheer him on. I needed to go to the restroom, so of course all three of us stood in the line to use one of the many portable toilets. When it was my turn, I discovered there was no latch in the one I was using. I instructed the kids to stand outside and hold the door shut. "When I knock on the door, then you can open it up," I said.

As soon as I was seated, Jason went around in back of the outhouse and launched into one of his drumming routines on the wall. Jodi, hearing the thumping, threw the door wide open. Hello, world! That incident put a serious crimp in Jason's drumming career.

Jason now uses his knowledge of drumming to pursue his interest in the guitar, and Jodi plays a mean CD.

3. Singing or art lessons. The mere appreciation of the arts gives children a sense of culture and history. They also allow another outlet for creative expression.

4. Karate, swimming, skating, horseback riding, bicycling, hockey, gymnastics. There is no end to physical activities that help children develop balance, coordination, and stamina. It's important for kids to learn about fitness and good health. As they get older, keeping in shape depends on their commitment to regular exercise.

There were no public pools, sidewalks, or gyms in our small town. I taught my own kids to swim at a motel pool in a neighboring town while my in-laws were visiting. Skating was limited to an annual school trip to a rink 40 miles away, and I drove Jodi to gymnastic lessons about 20 miles down the road.

Horses, on the other hand, were in abundance at our place. Each of us had our own. Although Jason wasn't at all interested in becoming a horseman, he was given no choice. When he was 7, Barry bought him a beautiful dun

Raising Kids Right

mare named Babe. Most kids I know would have given their trading card collection for such a steed, but not Jason. To Dad's chagrin, Jason was afraid of horses, and the tears flowed every time there was a riding session. Finally Barry gave up and relinquished the responsibility to me.

I coaxed and cajoled. I begged and pleaded. I patiently proceeded through each skill. Slowly Jason began to ride with a small amount of confidence. One day a pretty high school girl rode by our house on horseback. She had been one of my students, so she stopped in. Jason thought she was wonderful, and hung around to visit. Before she left, I had hired her to teach Jason to ride.

The following weekend she rode to our house, and Jason joined her for a trail ride through the hills. There were no tears. In fact, he couldn't get ready fast enough. After a few months, when his teacher quit to take on a new job, Jason was happy to hit the trail with other friends. Over time he won a boxful of ribbons at local gymkhanas and received a trophy for "most improved rider."

When his interest waned, we helped him set goals. He wanted a nice Western vest. I told him that 60 hours of horseback riding would get him the vest. We made a chart, and he wrote down his hours every time he rode. At first he accumulated an hour here and an hour there. Then he realized that at the rate he was going, he would never get the vest by winter. Now in earnest, he begin to log four and five hours at a time and soon had the vest. After 60 hours he and Babe were an inseparable team. Jason went on to learn a little about roping and team roped in a rodeo with Barry. (They didn't win—in fact, they didn't even catch the steer.)

"I prayed I wouldn't miss," said Jason.

As it turned out, Barry was the one who missed, so Jason didn't have to worry.

Free Time?

I felt a little guilty about forcing Jason to learn a skill that he didn't want to learn. But without some horse savvy he was never going to be able to establish a relationship with his stepdad.

Then I read a book by James Dobson, *Hide or Seek*. In it he told a story about a boy whose father forced him to learn to play tennis, and how painful it was. In the end, the boy was an accomplished tennis player. When other kids were getting into trouble, he had an identity. He knew he was the best tennis player in high school (or something like that). Dobson urged parents to teach their children any skill they could that would add to their repertoire.

It started out as a painful experience, but the results were good. Jason realized that we wouldn't give up on him, and that we would offer a variety of ways to accomplish the desired goal.

Then there was Jodi. While Jason had to be prodded and pushed to learn to ride, Jodi was *praying* for a pony. One morning she woke us with her squeals from the dining room.

"Mom! Dad! Come in here and look. There's a *pony* in the backyard!"

We joined her at the sliding-glass door, thinking she was trying to pull a joke on us. To our surprise, there stood a little caramel-colored pony. "He answered my prayer," Jodi whispered as she opened the door and slipped out. We were amazed ("O ye of little faith!"), but Jodi was satisfied that God had been the donor.

By midday the neighbors from down the road showed up, looking for their pony. When they saw how thrilled Jodi was with her gift from heaven, they decided their children were too big for the pony and gave her to Jodi. She

Raising Kids Right

immediately named it Dusty Candy and begged Barry to put together some tack for her.

Then when Jason became too long-legged for Babe, Jodi gave Dusty to some smaller kids down the road, and Babe was hers. She loved to ride and amassed quite a collection of ribbons and awards from the competitions she entered. Her daredevil attitude gave her the opportunity to experience numerous spills, but she always got back on for more.

The difference between Jason and Jodi's personalities called for a different approach to almost everything—Jason, being the careful one, and Jodi, who rushed ahead to try anything. When it came to swimming, I had to coax Jason again. "Jason, I'll give you a dollar if you swim to me." Or "Hey, Jason, I'll give you a dollar if you'll swim across the pool."

All the while, Jodi was jumping into the water and thrashing fearlessly about, yelling, "Hey, Mom, look at me! . . . *Glub, glub* . . . Look at me!" Just being at the swimming pool was reinforcement enough for her.

"That's great, Jodi! Do it again!" I'd yell back.

She still resents the fact that she got the fame, while Jason got the fortune! He tells her he was simply a smarter negotiator. And she tells him he was a con artist. They laugh about it, but the main thing is that they both learned to be good swimmers.

5. After-school enrichment programs. These programs usually challenge students intellectually. Projects call for research, creativity, and learning beyond the classroom curriculum. There are more opportunities for using technology and exploration. Jason got experience in oil painting, computers, and photography in an enrichment class.

6. Pop Warner football, cheerleading, Little League, baseball, girls' softball, soccer league. Nationally organized

Free Time?

sports leagues have set their roots into almost every little town in the country.

When Jason played Pop Warner football, Jodi was a cheerleader. Every day we ventured to a neighboring town for practice. It wasn't unusual to take other participants from our town. One day several kids called, asking for rides. By the time we arrived at practice, there were 11 of us crammed in my little yellow Toyota Corolla hatchback—six boys in full football gear and helmets, interspersed with four cheerleaders with pom-poms—all trying not to touch each other. The coach squinted in disbelief as we entered the parking lot.

"Here comes half the team . . . and they're all in one car." I jokingly patted the Bible on the dash and assured him we were in safe hands.

After the first game I looked for something in the newspaper about their defeat. Nothing. So the second week I took my camera and started writing Erma Bombeck-style Pop Warner coverage for the local weekly newspaper. It was the first writing I did for which I was actually paid.

Barry came to the games to cheer, so the whole family was involved.

7. Bible study or church activities. This is a good place for children to spend time, learning and having fun, under adult supervision in a Christian setting.

We had an evening youth group. Two of my friends and I planned the worship and curriculum. On a regular basis we took the kids to rallies and concerts. There were a couple concerts, Christian or not, during which I sat with my hands clamped over my ears, praying for silence. I stuffed cotton in my ears and read a book at one, but the kids thought the music was rad.

8. Child-care center or baby-sitter. When both parents are

Raising Kids Right

working, an on-site child-care center at the school or nearby location may be the only solution. Centers offer adult supervision, peer companionship, snacks, arts and crafts, enrichment, organized creative activities, outdoor play, and more. After directing five of them, I definitely see their advantage over letting children go home and stay alone.

Some families are blessed to have a nearby relative or a reliable baby-sitter. The warmth of a private home seems less desirable, however, if the child merely goes there to lie in front of a TV set. There are better options.

9. Pathfinders, Girl Scouts, Pioneer Girls, Blue Birds, Royal Rangers, Boy Scouts, etc. These organizations teach children life skills, giving them opportunities they wouldn't have otherwise. My kids spent a few happy years in scouting.

10. Parent's place of work. I wouldn't recommend taking your kids to work unless there is a designated place for them or special provisions to accommodate them. One summer when my children were small, I took a job as a dispatcher for a concrete pumping company. The owner ran his business from his home that included a nice enclosed yard. I accepted the job with the understanding that I could bring my children. Not many working mothers have that luxury, but more and more businesses are looking for ways to offer child care on the premises, or nearby.

I also sold real estate in the summers for a few years. The kids were big enough to stay alone, but it seemed like tempting fate to leave them. So I took them with me, if they had no other plans. Jodi used to go on caravans with the agents and me. She carried a fistful of my business cards and distributed them everywhere. By the time she was 8 years old, she could figure out down payments, read a monthly mortgage calculator, and navigate with the help of a Thomas Guide.

Free Time?

One day we were showing a home to a family. We had agreed that her job would be to keep the children occupied outside so that I could talk business with the parents inside. Jodi was a pro at entertaining, but she outdid herself that day. The prospective buyers' daughter had an artificial arm. Jodi was so curious about it that she launched a barrage of questions and wasn't a bit shy about asking the girl if she could take it off. By the time I got outside, Jodi was waving the artificial limb at me from around the side of the house, to the amusement of her new friend.

However, there were times my plan backfired. One day I had floor time in the real estate office and decided to take both kids and two of their friends to the shopping area where I worked. The boys took along skateboards, and the girls took skates. They went to the loading zone behind the building and entertained themselves by creating their own style of competition. I had promised them lunch at the local fast food spot if they would keep busy until noon.

Just at lunchtime a long-winded customer called for information. There was no end to his questions. Suddenly there was a ruckus in the back of the office, and four kids came skating through.

"Isn't it about time for lunch, Mom?" Jodi squealed as they flew by my desk and out the front door.

Raising children is a full-time job. Watching, nurturing, encouraging, planning, and loving takes a lot of concentration and energy. All too soon they will be grown and gone. Give them as many opportunities to experience life as you can. They are your estate to leave to the world.

Try this: Let your children know about all the choices of free-time activities available in your area. Encourage them to choose at least one. When the choice is made, let them

Raising Kids Right

know that this is a one-year commitment. At the end of the year either a new or an additional choice may be made. Commit yourself to doing everything necessary to help your child keep that commitment. Be as involved as you can be.

"Through idleness of the hands the house droppeth through." Ecclesiastes 10:18.

CHAPTER EIGHTEEN

Fitting Friends?

Your child will be influenced by peer pressure. Whether negatively or positively, he/she *will* be influenced. From an early age, there are some steps you can take that may help your child associate with people who can accentuate the positive.

Find a family-oriented church with a full youth program. As you make friends there, your children will meet other Christian children and will learn biblical principles.

Encourage commitment to the activities listed in chapter 15. This kind of involvement gives your child a better chance of meeting friends whose parents are interested in commitment and wholesome, planned activities.

Make friends with people who have similar interests, moral standards, and children the same ages as your own. This may take some searching, but the rewards are great. When you get together, the children have friends to play with while you visit with the parents. It makes mini-trips and recreation so much more fun. There are many advantages—and no disadvantages that I can think of.

We had friends whose two boys and two girls were near

the age of our children. In the summer, we would rent a houseboat on Lake Mead for three or four days. (The kids were a great asset when it came to loading and unloading supplies!) During the day they swam, fished, skied, ate, and provided entertainment with their antics. At night they all slept on the roof under the stars, giggling, making lots of noise, and having a great time. Visit the parents of your child's friends to get acquainted and to check out the situation. Before allowing your child to play at someone else's house, you'll want to know their standards for their children and their idea of supervision. If you don't feel satisfied that your child will be closely supervised, invite the friend to your home instead. Don't take any chances.

I have a friend who has eight children. Their backyard is huge, designed for kids. There is plenty of equipment, plus a concrete area for skating, basketball, etc. When anyone (guest or resident) misbehaves, they are benched for five minutes.

While I was visiting one day, I heard a neighbor calling over the fence for one of her children to come home. My friend stuck her head out the door and cheerfully called out, "She'll be there in three minutes, when her bench time is up." All the neighbors and their children knew her system and respected it.

Teach your child that a friend is someone who adds to your life. Show him/her how to evaluate the friendship by deciding if the relationship adds or subtracts. If it subtracts, causes your child to go against what is right, or causes a wedge between parents and child, then it is not a healthy friendship.

If you have told your children that they cannot go to a certain entertainment and their friends convince them that you are very narrow-minded and persuade them to go

Fitting Friends?

anyway, these are friends your children don't need. Help them to evaluate what these friendships are causing them to do, rather than making angry accusations about the friends. Help them to see that these friendships are subtracting from them and will not help them grow.

My son went through school with a couple boys he liked a great deal, but they both had fathers who drank excessively. He didn't feel comfortable staying overnight in their homes. When either of them would call to ask him over, he would say, "Mom, can I stay over night with ———?" Then he would cover the mouthpiece of the phone and whisper, "Say no. I'd rather have him come over here."

Teaching children to stick by their standards, when that means sacrificing their being part of the group, is difficult. I used to tell the children how easily trash flowed downstream with the current. We see the results of this concept in every polluted waterway. On the other hand, walking upstream, against the current, is never easy, just rewarding. It sometimes seems as though we Christians are walking alone, but when we reach the source of the spring of living water, we will know it was worthwhile.

Try this: Take time to know your children's friends and their families. Do what you can to develop family friendships.

"Blessed is the man that endureth temptation: for when he is tried, he shall receive the crown of life, which the Lord hath promised to them that love him." James 1:12.

CHAPTER NINETEEN

"Mom, Tell Jason to Stop Buggin' Me!"

Any family that has more than one child knows the phrase "sibling rivalry," the natural jealousy between two children. Child number one has front stage and Mom and Dad's undivided attention until Child number two comes along. It's only natural that Number one feels a bit upstaged for a while—sometimes for a lifetime.

Regardless of the reason, not many children go through life without some conflicts with siblings. Jason and Jodi were great friends; however, they still had their moments of conflict. "Mom, make Jason stop bugging me!" or "Jason, don't do that!" There's a time to stay back and see if they can work out the difficulty together, but when it escalates to screaming or hitting, then it's time to step in.

I had a short season of visiting a child psychologist when my children were little. And it was the best money I ever spent. He taught me a simple system that was useful and brought almost instant results.

Break the problem down
   1. What is the child doing that I don't want him/her to do?

"Mom, Tell Jason to Stop Buggin' Me!"

2. What do I want the child to do instead?

For the sake of discussion, let's say fighting is the problem. To answer the first question, I didn't want them fighting. And second, I wanted them to play peacefully together. Pretty simple so far, right? Then I had to modify my behavior in order to modify their behavior by:

1. Weakening my response to what I did not want them to do.
2. Rewarding the behavior I wanted.
3. Making sure the kids knew the plan.

Is that simple, or what? Well, not as simple as it sounds, but I can tell you it gets more natural the more you do it.

Before I began to use this system, I needed to explain to the kids exactly how it would go, so they understood what my expectations were and what an appropriate response would be.

I told them I would no longer tolerate fighting. When they did fight, they would have a five-minute time-out. When they played peacefully, I reinforced that behavior with a positive response or reward.

The System

In order to weaken my response to fighting, I could not go into a room screaming, swinging a dish towel, knocking kids around, and giving rapid-fire lectures. Instead, I entered the room and said in a calm voice, "Time-out." No lecture, no ranting, no raving—just a simple statement. They went to their own rooms, shut the doors, and I set the timer on the stove for five minutes. In five minutes they heard the oven buzzer go off and were welcome to come out and resume play. No lecture, no angry words, no reprimands.

What had I told them? That fighting was inappropriate behavior and I would not tolerate it. It gave them—*and* me—a chance to take a break, but no one had been demeaned. My kids liked to play together, and the separation wasn't much fun, so after a few separations they learned that there were better ways to work things out between themselves and forgo the isolation ward.

The hard part is really the easy part, but the part that's most forgotten and most important. *Reward the behavior you want!* The moment I realized the kids were playing peacefully together, I would step into the room and say something like, "It's great to see you kids playing together peacefully and enjoying each other's company." I might even chat with them for a few minutes to show them that I was willing to take time from my work to experience their good behavior.

Positive praise for anything will reinforce that behavior. The statement should be made when the good behavior is happening or immediately following. As soon as we would get into the car after visiting friends and the kids had behaved well, I would say, "I really appreciated your behavior at the Joneses' home. I was so proud of you both." The children would beam and say "Thanks," and I would be assured that the next time we visited they would remember how much I appreciated their good behavior. The trick is to reinforce *all* good behavior with positive responses.

Some parents are afraid to mention "good" behavior. They figure if everything is going well, why not leave it alone? Sometimes that's exactly why children misbehave; it's the only way to get Mom and/or Dad's attention. Then Mom and/or Dad reinforce the bad behavior by giving it their full and undivided attention.

The next time you observe a problem (only one at a time) developing in one of your children, think, *What is he/she doing that I don't want her to do?* and *What do I want*

"Mom, Tell Jason to Stop Buggin' Me!"

him/her to do in place of that? Write it down, and decide how to weaken the first and reinforce the second.

Then tell the child the plan. For example: "I'm not going to argue with you anymore when I give you no for an answer. I also will not give you an answer without thinking carefully first. But when I say no, I will expect you to accept that. If you want to discuss it, we can, but if you whine, cry, beg, or throw a fit, you will take a five-minute time-out in your room."

Now the hard part. The very next time I tell the child no to something and he/she accepts my answer, I need to say, "I really appreciate you trusting my judgment and accepting my answer." It would be a great chance to throw in an extra hug.

Try this: The next time you are aware that your children are doing something that is appropriate behavior that you like, be sure to reinforce it by telling them so. Repeat that reinforcement whenever you have the chance.

"Lo, children are an heritage of the Lord: and the fruit of the womb is his reward." Psalm 127:3.

CHAPTER TWENTY

Are You Listening to Me?

Kids need to hear and be heard. Have you ever thought about how much time your child spends talking to your knee, your thigh, or your elbow? It's not always easy to stop what you're doing and listen attentively. But it's important.

Think of your child, looking up at your back while you wash dishes or cook dinner, talking to your elbow as you nod your head and say "Uh-huh" or "Huh-uh" once in a while. Sit down on the kitchen floor sometime and try to carry on a conversation with your husband, and you'll see how out of touch you feel.

It's easy to allow distractions to rob us of quality time with the children. I know that between preparing dinner and correcting papers, I spent too much time on the phone, talking with my friends. At least when I was correcting papers on the sofa I was facing the right direction, and the kids felt free to sit and talk about school, friends, sports, or whatever.

Telephone conversations shut out children; if they are going to misbehave, it will be while you are stuck to the end of the telephone receiver. I remember trying to carry on a phone conversation while Jason and Jodi emptied the

Are You Listening to Me?

dishwasher. They were goofing around and being silly. Jason took the basket filled with silverware out of the dishwasher and, instead of plucking each piece out and sorting it, turned the whole thing upside down in the drawer. As the silverware went crashing into the drawer, the two of them dissolved into hysterical laughter. I was trying to counsel a friend who had a serious problem, and the clatter was deafening. The two of them still talk about how I came after them, ineffectively waving a towel.

Of course, hearing is a two-way street. There was a period of time when we were sure Jason was going deaf. He'd be busy playing a video game or watching TV and couldn't hear a thing.

"Jason, would you please take the garbage out?"

H'mmm. He must not have heard me.

A little louder. "Jason, how about taking the garbage out?"

Still no response. So I'd walk to the video controls to exercise my ability to use the "off" button. When the machine fell silent, he'd look at me and say, "Huh?"

I decided to conduct a little experiment. The next time I asked him to do something, and got no response, I quietly murmured, "How about some ice cream?" Guess what? He answered immediately. We decided we needn't have his hearing tested after all.

Try this: Take a moment each day to sit down or somehow get on eye level with your child. Then listen and enjoy.

"He that hath ears to hear, let him hear." **Matthew 11:15.**

CHAPTER TWENTY-ONE

What Are You Listening To?

Whether it is the radio, tapes, concerts, CDs, or videos, sooner or later your children will discover music beyond what they learn in church and school. Will you allow them free choice? Or will you help them make choices?

When Jason was about 10, he became interested in a certain rock and roll group. They wore black costumes and painted their faces black and white in a grotesque and mystical way that seemed to attract the teenyboppers. Jason had several of their albums. Then when he was 12 he accepted Jesus as his personal Saviour and decided to live a life that was pleasing to God. Right away he began to look at the sinister faces of the rock and roll group and doubt their motives. He listened carefully to the lyrics and found that their songs promoted a philosophy that could not be supported biblically.

I wanted him to learn that God can fill us up with good things in place of things of the world. But asking a 12-year-old kid to throw away his albums might cause him to think that God took things away from us. So I took Jason to a great Christian bookstore where customers could listen to

What Are You Listening To?

tapes (this was before CDs) on headsets. I offered to buy any tapes or albums he wanted in trade for his rock and roll albums. He got the Christian music, and I got his albums, which I disposed of. Everyone was happy. It was the first step in learning that for everything the world offers, God offers something better and more pleasing.

There is plenty of Christian music that though raucous enough to be objectionable to adults, is radical enough to satisfy teenagers. So take them to the nearest Christian bookstore to shop. My kids loved to invite a carload of friends to go with us to Christian concerts where the music sometimes made me cover my ears in chagrin, but the message that followed caused the kids to open their hearts to the Lord. They laughed at me as I anguished at the racket, but seeing them come to know Jesus made it all a "joyful noise" to me.

We had a house rule at home that music should be a one room affair. If it became distracting to someone in another room, it needed to be turned down.

Try this: The next time you see, or hear, your child listening to music, ask what he/she is listening to. Ask what the words mean. Do the words support Christian beliefs? Why, or why not?

"They lifted up their voice with the trumpets and cymbals and instruments of musick, and praised the Lord." 2 Chronicles 5:13.

CHAPTER TWENTY-TWO

Have You Done Your Chores?

What constitutes a chore? My old Webster's calls it "a small or odd job; the regular or daily light work of a household or farm." There were always plenty of chores to do in the country. Our kids did everything from bottle-feed calves to preparing chickens to make the transition from the barn to the frying pan. They herded cows and helped with roundup, but not as often as they set the table, washed dishes, and took out the trash.

Doing chores is just another part of being a member of a family. Everyone needs to pitch in and do what needs to be done. But there are some wrinkles to work out. If you assign chores to certain individuals, invariably the next time that chore needs to be done the assignee will be gone to a ball game. If you pay children for doing chores, they get the idea they should be paid for anything and everything. If you, as parents, do all the chores because it's easier than getting the children to do them, the children will always expect you to do them. If you make charts to keep track of completed chores, you will probably overlook a few. Then when you ask them to do something that is not on the list,

Have You Done Your Chores?

they'll reply, "It's not in my job description."

I used the "twice nice" rule. I would ask twice, nicely, and if I didn't get action I headed for the paddle. That usually got results, because I didn't use the paddle often. And if I had it to do over, there would be *no* paddle. A spank with the hand is painful enough and shouldn't happen often (if you consistently use your reinforcement system), and *never* should be done in anger. I always told the kids how much I appreciated everything they did, whether it was setting the table or feeding the horses when Barry was away.

So what's the answer? Perhaps there isn't a comprehensive one.

Try this: Always ask kindly, and express gratitude when the job is finished.

"Well done, thou good and faithful servant: thou hast been faithful over a few things, I will make thee ruler over many things." Matthew 25:21.

CHAPTER TWENTY-THREE

What's for Dinner?

I didn't do a good job of teaching my children to cook. Like my mother, I figured if they hung around in the kitchen long enough they would surely see how it was done. I was always moving at warp speed and was the self-proclaimed queen of the 10-minute meal.

When the children were small, we lived in a tiny old house and ate at a card table. It was cozy. Then when Jason was 7 and Jodi was 4, we moved to a mobile home and ate at a curved bar facing the stove. I served each plate right out of the steaming pots and handed them to each family member, just like a fry cook in a greasy spoon. We took turns blessing the food.

One family we knew took their places at the table. Then each person would raise a finger in the air, and the last person to raise his or her finger had to say grace. It was cute, but I always felt that God deserved a bit more respect. In fact, it should be an honor to be the one to praise Him and give thanks for His abundant blessings.

Dinnertime was always a time of conversation. We talked about school, work, and anything that went on dur-

What's for Dinner?

ing the day. There were times when we discussed difficult topics that were not conducive to digestion. If conversation waned, we took turns starting new topics or would make up trivia questions to try to stump one another. Usually, we weren't in a hurry to leave the table.

Since I served the plates, it's safe to say my children didn't have much choice about their portions. Everyone got a little bit of everything, and each was expected to eat it. That was the way *I* was raised. Every meal consisted of a glass of milk, salad or fruit, rice or potatoes, a vegetable, and meat (sometimes a casserole).

I went to one cooking class in my life, and the only thing I learned was to serve a variety of colors and something from each food group. Consequently, I think our meals were well balanced. The rule about eating everything on your plate still stumps me. I'm not sure it's healthy. Yes, it teaches your children to eat everything and not be picky, but to this day I can't leave a scrap on my plate without seeing the faces of those starving children in China.

I told the family, "If you don't eat it tonight, you'll see it again tomorrow." Leftovers weren't fed to the pets; they *were* the next night's meal. One night I said, "You've got to eat this stuff, or I'll have to throw it away."

Jodi caught me. "Wait a minute, Mom. If this stuff is so close to rotten that the only other logical place for it is the garbage can, why are you trying to feed it to us?"

Good point. But "waste not, want not," my mother always said.

The most common problem I heard from parents about dinnertime concerned children spilling things. That wasn't a common occurrence at our house for two reasons. For one thing, as we sat at the bar, we all faced the same general direction. The only things we passed back and forth

Raising Kids Right

were salt and butter. The main reason, however, was we taught the kids where their drinking glass belonged—at the upper right side of the plate. When they finished taking a drink, they put it back in that place.

Our manners were not extremely polished, but "Please" and "Thank you" were required. Utensils were properly used, a napkin was in every lap, but I have to admit that even *I* put an elbow on the table after a hard day.

It all seems so simple, but I'm reminded that some folks allow their children to bounce from here to there during dinner. Others leave the TV blasting and drag trays of food to the family room. There are families who don't even sit down together and eat. That's a shame. Dinner should, and can, be a pleasant time that everyone anticipates.

Try this: Eat dinner with everyone seated together. Make it a time of sharing and fellowship for the family. Turn the TV off.

"Bless thine inheritance: feed them also, and lift them up for ever." Psalm 28:9.

CHAPTER TWENTY-FOUR

In Case of an Emergency

I never realized how important emergency drills were until I woke up one morning to find our house full of smoke. It poured up from the baseboards, and flames flickered under the flooring where they could not be seen or extinguished.

My first thought was of the children. As I threw open their door, a cloud of smoke poured out. Both kids were asleep—or unconscious. We'll never know which, because we carried them out of the house and locked them in the car for safety. Their nostrils were lined with soot, which showed they had been breathing smoke for a period of time. The fresh air revived them, and we felt blessed.

I had planned a class field trip to San Juan Capistrano that day. The bus driver, who was chief of the volunteer fire department, had asked me to make a thermos of coffee for him, so I had set the alarm 45 minutes earlier than usual to allow plenty of time to prepare it. That early alarm saved us all from dying in the smoke-filled house. (Or was it the Lord God who knows all things and knew that someday we'd tell the story to His glory?)

Later, when I told the fire chief how long it took to find

Raising Kids Right

the phone number in the book (this was before 911), he scolded me for not having the number at my fingertips. When I got home from the field trip, there was the sticker with the emergency number—right on my phone. I had been too rattled to see it, and we had never practiced any emergency procedures.

At school your kids will practice fire and earthquake drills on a regular basis. It's a good idea to do the same at home. You may feel stupid doing this at first, but you will feel worse if an emergency happens and you have no plan. Fire can happen to anyone, and in southern California, so can earthquakes.

Try this: Make a diagram of your home and property. With your children, make an emergency plan. Decide with them how to get out of their rooms, where to go to meet, how to wake others, and how to call for emergency services.

"Behold, how great a matter a little fire kindleth!" James 3:5.

CHAPTER TWENTY-FIVE

Have You Finished Your Homework?

Every now and then I meet a man who was once a little boy in my class many years before. He always reminds me that the only time he ever did his homework was when he lived in our home.

His house had burned down that year, and his family had lost everything except their lives. We offered to have Kenny come and stay with us until his family could find another place. He was clothed, fed, and made to feel like part of the family.

Barry gave him the job of setting the table and promoted Jodi to dishwasher. Kenny was one of four children, so he thought it was pretty quiet at our house. What impressed him most, though, was that every night, just after dinner, both kids would file out to their rooms and do their homework without being asked.

"Come on, Kenny, time to do homework so we can hear a story," they'd coax.

With Jason's help they'd be finished in no time.

Homework should be as much a natural part of the routine as brushing teeth. Just as teeth brushing begins when children get teeth, doing homework should start as soon as they have homework.

Let me put on my schoolteacher hat for a moment. Many parents have caused a big rift at home because of homework. Some homework is meant just for the child, while some is to be a shared experience, and some is for the parent only.

Homework just for the child might be math problems that are done to reinforce what was learned in class that day. If the parent does the problems the kids don't learn anything. If the parent hassles the kid to hurry up and do it, the experience is going to be negative, and the responsibility is on the parent. The child is not taking responsibility, and this will turn into a bad scene that will be repeated nightly.

Drilling on spelling words is something the parent can enter into by giving the child the words. But the child can write the words five times each without anyone's help.

Some assignments ask the parent to take part. Besides learning together, it is the school's effort to get families to do more bonding. An admirable concept. These are usually "no-fail" assignments, but your child will be let down if you don't participate.

The assignments that are just for parents might include filling out forms, agreeing to participate in some activity, writing a note to tell why the child was absent, supplying cookies for a class party, and more.

The main thing is to be positive. Help your child set goals, and reward the meeting of those goals. Make a chart so your child can check off homework when it is finished. Set a goal with the child that you both agree he/she can attain. When it is attained and rewarded, then think about a new goal that stretches your child just a little. It's important not to frustrate a child by setting goals that are too high.

Have You Finished Your Homework?

If you have a child who drags his/her feet and needs more encouragement, make the goals smaller. Number the chart to reflect the goal. Every time your child completes three or four problems, he/she can come out of his room and have you check the problems. If the problems are correct, give the child a star before he/she continues. When that becomes too easy, extend the goal by asking for more problems to be done before the chart is marked. If one or more problems are incorrect, it is time to help—not by doing the problem, but by asking questions that will lead the child to get to the right answers.

If rewards don't work, set the goal so it is more attainable. Either make the task smaller, the length of time shorter, or the reward more enticing. Some parents tell their children, "If you get all A's on your report card I'll take you to Disneyland." If the child has never had an A this goal is out of reach, and he/she will give up before getting started.

I wanted my children to get A's and B's, if they could. I could accept a C, but then it was definitely time to research more thoroughly and find out how they could improve. Getting a D meant it was time to get a tutor and cut out other activities until there was improvement.

If your children are older and gold stars, treats, quarters, and toys don't work anymore, set up a different plan. The reward will be the opportunity to continue participation in extracurricular activities. Anything below a C grade will constitute taking away those privileges.

One Christian counselor joked, "Tell your son that if he gets passing grades he will be allowed to live another year."

I have worked with so many parents who have lavished gifts on their children from day one. They seem to be buying their favor. Maybe they feel guilty about not being at

Raising Kids Right

home enough, so any material thing the kid wants is purchased. Then when they can't figure out how to motivate the kid to do homework or get better grades, they are stymied. What message have they given junior? "You can do whatever you want and still get piles of goodies." And suddenly they have no leverage.

I'd rather see a child get a gift because of good performance at school or some admirable accomplishment. Remember, this is the same mom talking whose son had to ride a horse for 60 hours to earn a vest. What did he learn? If you want something bad enough, you better be willing to put in time and effort to earn it.

Try this: Make a chart for your child. On the nights his/her homework is finished before family reading time, he/she gets a gold star. Psychologists say that you need to do something only 21 days in a row and it will become a habit.

If your children have already become responsible for their own homework, don't bother with the chart. You have already instilled the importance of personal achievement in them. Tell them how proud you are of the way they take care of their own responsibilities.

"That the Lord thy God may bless thee in all the work of thine hand which thou doest." Deuteronomy 14:29.

CHAPTER TWENTY-SIX

Nighttime TV?

When is there time for TV in the evening? With dinner, homework, chores, family reading, and bedtime, who has time? And if you did have time, what would you watch that would be good for kids?

When I was a kid, there was *I Love Lucy, Leave It to Beaver, Father Knows Best, Ozzie and Harriet,* and *Donna Reed.* Family shows about family values. Few programs offer good, clean, moral fun anymore. That's one of the reasons we had family reading time. It was *always* better than TV.

There was a little time after chores while I was fixing dinner that the kids had time to watch a program, but later than that Barry had the remote control and it was hopeless. One of the things we liked to do instead of TV was dream up competitive games to test each other's intelligence, strength, endurance, or agility.

We discouraged the celebration of Halloween at our house, but we always had the big pumpkin contest. Barry would bring home two big pumpkins. The four of us would guess their weights, heights, circumferences, scoops of goop inside, and number of seeds. The guesses would be

Raising Kids Right

written on a chart. Then Barry and Jason would weigh, measure, cut, scoop, and count the seeds of their pumpkin while Jodi and I did the same with ours. We gave points for the closest guesses and ascertained a winner by totaling the points. I don't remember what the winner got, but I do remember we all had a lot of fun.

When the contest was over, we cut faces and made jack-o'-lanterns and baked the seeds to eat. One time we cut the pumpkins up and made pies. Another time I made a facial out of the goop by packing the slimy stuff on my face.

Then there was the time we had our own Olympics. We went outside for a jump and reach contest to see who could jump the highest above their reach and made a mark with a piece of chalk. Jodi and I always won the jump rope contest, but the men did better at the mile jog.

One night we had a sit-ups contest. Jodi and I pooped out early, but Barry and Jason continued. Neither would give in. Their faces grew beet red as they pumped up and down. When we saw blood oozing through Jason's pants, we finally convinced them to quit simultaneously. He had worn a quarter-size patch of skin off his behind.

Try this: Exercise your right to shut the TV off and do something else that's more fun. Play a game with your kids, read together, or make up fun things to do.

Watch your TV guide for good, clean entertainment. Watch a program only if you have selected it. Don't leave the TV on without planning what you're going to watch.

"And ye shall rejoice before the Lord your God, ye, and your sons, and your daughters." Deuteronomy 12:12.

CHAPTER TWENTY-SEVEN

Family Meetings

When there was a tough issue that needed to be discussed, we planned a family meeting. Unfortunately, these meetings usually resulted in someone being asked to change their behavior or being reprimanded for something that didn't get done. It always involved solving a problem. Anyone could add to the agenda, but when I announced a family meeting, both kids usually groaned in anticipation.

Our meetings weren't always negative, but for some reason the kids expected the worst. Our topics were pretty weighty, and it wasn't exactly a democracy. Everyone had an opinion, but we adults had the last word. We didn't call a family meeting to hand out praise; praise was given freely at other times. So I guess it was a dead giveaway, and the meetings were attended with fear and trepidation.

I still think the idea was good. We simply needed to make sure there were plenty of positive items on our agenda. We did usually see an issue through to a solution in those meetings, even if they were painful.

Raising Kids Right

Try this: Plan a family meeting, and let every family member put two things on the agenda. One of the items has to be a discussion about something positive.
"And they reasoned with themselves." Mark 11:31.

CHAPTER TWENTY-EIGHT

Let's Read Together

In the "old days," before TV and radio, families sat around the fire at night and read together. We decided that was the kind of atmosphere we wanted to create for our family. It meant that after dinner we kept the TV off and took the phone off the hook. Now, if you leave the phone off the hook, an alarm will sound to remind you to replace it. So you have to turn the phone off, unplug it, or trust the answering machine, set to answer quickly. Don't weaken and answer the phone! Keep the time uninterrupted.

We didn't have family reading every night, only on nights when everyone was home. If Barry went roping or I had a night class, we waited for a better night when we could all be together.

During our reading time the kids could sit wherever they were comfortable, as long as they sat quietly. They sprawled on the floor, lay on the sofa, lounged in beanbag chairs, or conformed to regular chair sitting. They always did better if they were out of arm and foot reach of each other. Then there was no temptation to engage in the "stop touching me" game.

Raising Kids Right

Twenty minutes is about the attention span of kids. Oddly enough, it's about as long as I could read aloud and Barry could keep from falling asleep on the sofa. Sometimes the kids would beg to continue if we were in an exciting part of the story. If Barry began to snore outrageously, we quit early.

I was the permanent reader. Not because I knew all the words, but because I read with expression and dramatized for effect. It made the story more fun for everyone. We read some great books. There are lists of the classics and "core novels" available at your child's school library. We chose mostly animal and family stories. I remember a few: *Old Yeller, Big Mutt, Call of the Wild, Where the Red Fern Grows, Incredible Journey, Little Britches, Little House on the Prairie,* and *Joni.*

Some of the stories were tear jerkers. We never did finish *Where the Red Fern Grows.* I had just read the book to my class and thought my tears were spent. Quite the opposite! I got choked up on page 1, just thinking about what was going to happen at the end. I had to quit reading 30 pages before the end and paraphrase the rest of the story, sobbing uncontrollably. I read it for 17 more years to my class, and I never could get through it without a few tears.

We started reading time at home when Jodi was 3 and Jason was 6 years old. When Jodi was 8, she accepted Jesus as her Saviour. Within the next four months Jason, Barry, and I asked Jesus to be Lord of our lives also.

Jason suggested at that time that we read some books of the Bible during family reading time. We used his copy of "The Word" Bible because it was a simplified paraphrased version everyone could understand.

After reading time we would take turns mentioning things we'd like to pray about. Then we would all join in

Let's Read Together

prayer, each praying for some of the needs that had been discussed, giving thanks for the many blessings of God, and asking for guidance and wisdom in the days to come.

We read more than 10 books of the Bible. By this time Jason was in Christian high school, where he had Bible study every day. So we changed our format again. I bought some Bible quiz books and typed up groups of 10 quiz questions. Instead of reading, each of us got a paper with the 10 questions for the night and used our study Bibles to see who could complete the quiz first. It was good practice in the use of the concordance, Bible encyclopedia, and chain references.

Try this: As a family, choose a book everyone will enjoy. Turn off the TV after dinner, turn off the phone, and enjoy reading a story filled with warmth and love. It's sure to offer more than prime-time TV.

"Oh, that my words were now written! oh, that they were printed in a book!" Job 19:23.

CHAPTER TWENTY-NINE

Now I Lay Me Down to Sleep

When a child comes to class in the morning and can't seem to focus, my first question is "What time did you go to bed last night?" The answer often tells the tale.

Children are active all day long. They use up more energy than adults and need far more sleep. They do not know instinctively when they should go to bed. Parents have to make that decision. An overly tired child may become grouchy, giddy, or uncontrollable. There are a few who will lie down and drop off to sleep on the spot.

When my two children were little, we visited friends in Santa Maria (the same ones from chapter 18, "Fitting Friends?") who had eight children, ranging from a newborn to a 15-year-old. All of them were wonderful children. Once dinner was over, they all took part in the cleanup detail. The adults retired to the living room while the children cleared the table, washed dishes, and cleaned up the kitchen. They even vacuumed the entire dining room and left a candle burning in the center of the table so that all was ready to serve dessert.

I marveled at the cooperation and organization of this

Now I Lay Me Down to Sleep

large family. As the evening wore on, a few of the children excused themselves and wandered off to bed. The others fell asleep here and there around the living room. One curled up on the sofa next to me, and another slept on the floor with her feet propped up on the TV set.

I thought this was rather strange, so I asked, "Are we disrupting your children's bedtime?"

"Oh, no," the father replied. He went on to explain that when he was a little boy his parents made him go to bed before he was ready, and that he didn't require much sleep. So he would take a flashlight to bed and read under the covers. He swore that he would never impose a bedtime on his children.

Interesting! And I must say it worked for them. I don't know how everyone finally got to bed. The living room had the appearance of a war zone, with bodies strewn here and there. Personally, I wouldn't want to pick up kids and deposit them in bed without baths, teeth brushing, and other bathroom business. It seemed unnatural (or perhaps too natural) to me.

We are all different, and our needs vary. Some parents choose their children's bedtime according to TV show times. For example, they'll say, "When *Full House* is over, you will go to bed."

Some choose a bedtime according to the child's grade in school, i.e., kindergartners go to bed at 8:00, third graders go to bed at 8:30, fifth graders go to bed at 9:00, and so on. What is right for your child? There isn't a standard time that is right for every child. The important thing is to have a rested and receptive student in the morning.

Some parents let their children stay up late in the summer. Consequently, there is little time for Mom and Dad's quiet time together, and the children are cranky during

Raising Kids Right

the months that should be fun and relaxing. They will enjoy summer and all the activity better if they have plenty of sleep.

When my children gave up naps and started school, it wasn't unusual for them to go to bed before it was dark outside. If your child is one who needs 12 hours of sleep, it will be a blessing to provide that opportunity—both to you and to him. The waking hours will be much happier for everyone.

When Jason was about 3 years old, I read a magazine article about tantrums. I still remember that it attributed tantrums to two causes—being either too tired or too frustrated with a task that had become too difficult.

It was about a week later that Jason got upset about a game he was playing and threw the game pieces—and his first tantrum. Having just read the article, I surmised that the game wasn't frustrating him, because he had played it many times and had it mastered. It hardly seemed possible that he could be too tired, since it was only about 5:30. At any rate, I picked him up and deposited him on his bed for a time-out. Five minutes later I went to the bedroom to invite him to come out, and he was fast asleep. That convinced me of the importance of sleep, and I don't remember him ever throwing another tantrum.

Visiting others at bedtime was enlightening. I had a friend who was mother to an active little boy. Her husband put him to bed each night, but when Daddy was out for the evening, the boy would not cooperate. The boy had his mother stymied and his dad was feeling frustrated. He attached a screen door with hinges to the top of the crib that could be latched down tight to keep the boy in bed. It seemed like cruel punishment to me, but they had waited too long to deal with the problem, and the child had become unmanageable.

Now I Lay Me Down to Sleep

In teaching parenting classes, I've found that bedtime presents unique problems in many families. Some parents say to their children, "If you do that again I'll put you to bed." Consequently, children think of going to bed as a punishment instead of a treat that is good for them. Hence, bedtime becomes a negative thing. You want the bedtime routine to be smooth and positive.

When a child reaches school age, it's important to keep a schedule that allows all the sleep your child needs. His/her success depends on it.

Try this: Put your children to bed at any time you choose. If they don't wake up by themselves in the morning, put them to bed 30 minutes earlier the next night. Keep using the process until you find a time that allows them to wake up easily at "rise and shine" time. When you find the best time, make that bedtime until it isn't appropriate anymore.

"When you lie down, you will not be afraid; when you lie down, your sleep will be sweet." Proverbs 3:24, NASB.

CHAPTER THIRTY

Can We Read a Little More?

When Jason and Jodi were getting ready for bed, I would often say, "If you get ready in time, you can read for a while before you turn the lights off."

Two things happened. First, reading was considered a treat and something wonderful to do before turning off the lights. Second, when they were ready to read, all the other chores and trips to the kitchen and bathroom were finished.

When my mother said, "It's time to go to bed," she might as well have said, "It's time for the beatings to begin." I saw bedtime as cruel and unusual punishment. I didn't like being in the dark, and I was never sleepy. Time after time I would call my mother back into our room for a kiss, a glass of water, a hug, prayers, or a discussion about some silly incident that happened during the day. Anything to stall the inevitable. When she would finally say, "And this is the last time I'm coming in," we knew there was no hope of her return unless we could convince her that our lives were endangered by some flesh-eating flying monster. Then she would send Dad in with a flyswatter.

Sleep would not come, and I would crawl down the hall

Can We Read a Little More?

on my belly to watch TV from behind the chair. I loved TV. In 1951 we had bought the second set in town. My fifth-grade teacher, Mrs. Van Hook, had the first one. She probably wished I'd spent more time with my schoolbooks.

I heard stories about children who loved to read and would sneak flashlights under the covers after lights out. Reading was a struggle for me, and I envied that skill in others. I decided when I became a mom I would do everything in my power to turn my children on to reading. So I made it a treat, a reward.

Try saying "Well, it looks like it's about bedtime. If you hurry and get your bath taken and your jammies on, you may read for 15 minutes before we turn the lights out."

Rather than "You have to read for 15 minutes," say "You get to read."

Not "You must read," but "You have the privilege of reading."

Jason and Jodi are both good readers and still consider it a treat when they have time to read. I would lie down on the bed with Jodi and sometimes read a few pages. We would evaluate the day and talk about tomorrow's schedule. We reminded each other about piano lessons, Girl Scouts, and ball practice. We would pray together, kiss, and say good night. When Jodi's light was out, I'd go into Jason's room, lie on his bed, and go through the same process. It was nearly always a pleasant time.

If you want to encourage your children to enjoy reading, take them to the store and pick out rewards that are affordable and healthy. Cut the treats into bite-size pieces and store them in a special place. Help your children set attainable goals: "If you read five pages you may have one piece of your treat." Our children loved the reading and the rewards along the way. It encouraged them to practice, practice, practice.

Raising Kids Right

How many of us read in order to make a transition from the concerns of the day to the restfulness of night? It works for kids, too. Their bodies slow down, and their eyelids become heavy.

Try this: Offer 15 minutes of reading to your children on the nights they get to bed early enough.

"Till I come, give attendance to reading." 1 Timothy 4:13.

CHAPTER THIRTY-ONE

God Bless One and All

In the last quiet moments, I loved to lie on the bed with Jodi and listen to her last thoughts of the day. Jodi is a talker, and sometimes she would try to keep me there as long as possible. She would pray aloud, thanking Jesus for everything, and asking Him to take care of everyone. I'd kiss her and tell her "nightee night," like my mom used to tell me.

Then it was Jason's turn. He always had a hard time getting to sleep. He seemed to have a lot to think about. Instead of counting sheep, he would pray for people by alphabetical order. One night he would pray only for people whose names started with A. The next night he prayed for the B's, and so on. If your name happened to be Zelda, it would have taken him a while to get to you.

One morning we heard that Robert, a brother of one of Jason's friends, had had an accident. He'd been trapped in his burning pickup truck. At the last second someone pulled him out to safety. Jason said, "I'm sure glad I was praying for the R's last night!"

We always talked about the plans for the next day,

Raising Kids Right

prayed, and kissed; then out went the light. Much later, when I was ready for bed, I'd go back into Jason's and Jodi's rooms. I'd kneel by each bed and thank God for them. I asked Him to prepare godly spouses for each of them, and prayed that they would glorify God with their lives.

Try this: Love your children with all your heart, pray with them every day, and pray over them every night.

"I will both lay me down in peace, and sleep: for thou, Lord, only makest me dwell in safety." Psalm 4:8.

EPILOGUE

When I started to write this book, our kids were young adults. Now they are both happily married. I don't know of anything that has been more gratifying to me as a parent than seeing them choose godly mates.

Jodi is head trainer and strength and fitness coach for the Ice Dogs hockey team at the Valley Ice Garden in Bozeman, Montana. Her husband, Rob Higgs, is head trainer for the Montana State University football team. They live too far away, but we reach them with our prayers and E-mail.

Jason is the product information specialist for Mitsubishi Motor Sales of America, and his wife, Cecillia, is a construction consultant. They bought a home only a mile from us, and we fellowship at the same church.

I asked both Jason and Jodi if there was anything they wanted to make sure I put in this book that would help parents in their child-rearing experience. Jason didn't comment, but Jodi sent this E-mail:

I guess I'd most want to stress that parents need to sacrifice in order to give their children every possible opportunity to succeed at something, be it sports, band, art, etc. People succeed because of opportunities, no matter how small or large they are. Children need to be involved in activities of their liking, and, if this begins at an early age, they won't be so likely to choose inappropriate lifestyles. Children need self-worth—to have some things they did, or made, or accomplished that they can really be proud of. I can't think of a time in my life when I wasn't

Raising Kids Right

striving for just that.

Getting my new job with the Ice Dogs is the most recent example. I needed to be known for something, even if it was only in my own mind. I needed to feel good about myself, especially after all the hard work my family and I put into the making of me.

Oh, one more thing: keep your eyes open for the rebuttal book, Raising Parents Right, Morning, Noon, and Night. *Ha!*